P9-CJX-986

TOM HERRING AND GRANDSON, J.T., AGE 2, REEL IN A NOT-SO-BIG ONE FROM FLORIDA'S SUWANNEE RIVER.

N.G.S. PHOTOGRAPHER GEORGE F. MOBLEY

AMERICA'S GREAT HIDEAWAYS

Prepared by the Special Publications Division   *National Geographic Society, Washington, D.C.*

RIDERS ENJOY A BACKCOUNTRY PANORAMA IN ALBERTA'S BANFF NATIONAL PARK.

SCOTT RUTHERFORD

AMERICA'S GREAT HIDEAWAYS

Contributing Authors: ERIK LARSON, THOMAS O'NEILL,
   CYNTHIA RUSS RAMSAY, JENNIFER C. URQUHART
Contributing Photographers: IRA BLOCK, MATT BRADLEY,
   STEPHEN R. BROWN, MIKE CLEMMER, GEORGE HERBEN,
   GEORGE F. MOBLEY, SCOTT RUTHERFORD

Published by THE NATIONAL GEOGRAPHIC SOCIETY
GILBERT M. GROSVENOR, *President*
MELVIN M. PAYNE, *Chairman of the Board*
OWEN R. ANDERSON, *Executive Vice President*
ROBERT L. BREEDEN, *Senior Vice President,*
   Publications and Educational Media

Prepared by THE SPECIAL PUBLICATIONS DIVISION
DONALD J. CRUMP, *Director*
PHILIP B. SILCOTT, *Associate Director*
BONNIE S. LAWRENCE, *Assistant Director*

Staff for this Book
PAUL MARTIN, *Managing Editor*
CHARLES E. HERRON, *Illustrations Editor*
MARIANNE R. KOSZORUS, *Art Director*
JODY BOLT, *Consulting Art Director*
AMY GOODWIN ALDRICH, *Project Coordinator*
SALLIE M. GREENWOOD, STEPHEN J. HUBBARD,
   TEE LOFTIN, *Senior Researchers*

LESLIE B. ALLEN, TOM MELHAM, H. ROBERT
   MORRISON, SUZANNE VENINO, *Picture Legend Writers*
JOHN D. GARST, JR., ROBERT W. CRONAN, JOSEPH F.
   OCHLAK, ISAAC ORTIZ, NANCY S. STANFORD,
   KEVIN Q. STUEBE, *Map Research and Production*
STUART E. PFITZINGER, *Illustrations Assistant*

Engraving, Printing, and Product Manufacture
ROBERT W. MESSER, *Manager*
DAVID V. SHOWERS, *Production Manager*
GEORGE J. ZELLER, JR., *Production Project Manager*
GREGORY STORER, *Senior Assistant Production Manager*
MARK R. DUNLEVY, *Assistant Production Manager*

TIMOTHY H. EWING, *Production Assistant*
MARY F. BRENNAN, VICKI L. BROOM, CAROL ROCHELEAU
   CURTIS, KATHERINE R. DAVENPORT, LORI E. DAVIE,
   MARY ELIZABETH DAVIS, ANN DI FIORE, ROSAMUND
   GARNER, BERNADETTE L. GRIGONIS, VIRGINIA W.
   HANNASCH, NANCY J. HARVEY, JOAN HURST, ARTEMIS
   S. LAMPATHAKIS, ANN E. NEWMAN, CLEO E. PETROFF,
   VIRGINIA A. WILLIAMS, *Staff Assistants*

TERESA P. BARRY, MAUREEN WALSH, *Indexers*

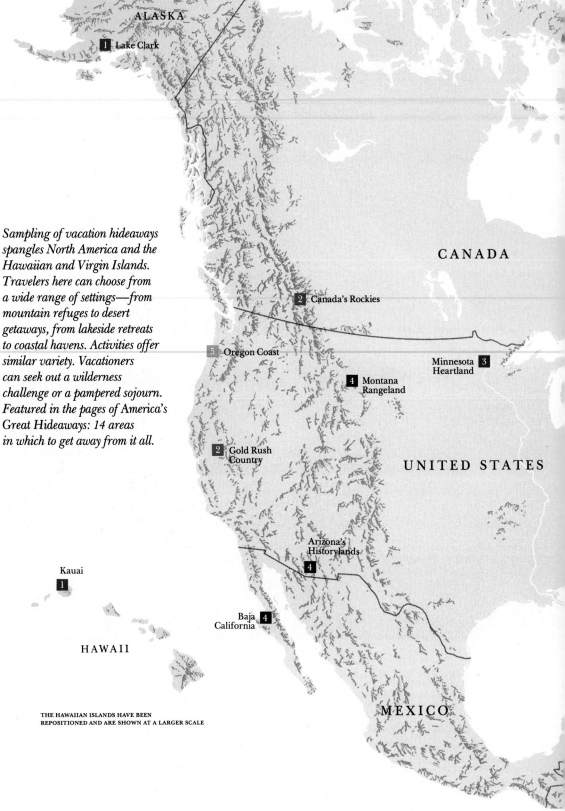

Sampling of vacation hideaways spangles North America and the Hawaiian and Virgin Islands. Travelers here can choose from a wide range of settings—from mountain refuges to desert getaways, from lakeside retreats to coastal havens. Activities offer similar variety. Vacationers can seek out a wilderness challenge or a pampered sojourn. Featured in the pages of America's Great Hideaways: 14 areas in which to get away from it all.

ALASKA

1 Lake Clark

CANADA

2 Canada's Rockies

5 Oregon Coast

Minnesota 3
Heartland

4 Montana
Rangeland

UNITED STATES

2 Gold Rush
Country

Arizona's
Historylands
4

Kauai

1

Baja 4
California

HAWAII

MEXICO

THE HAWAIIAN ISLANDS HAVE BEEN
REPOSITIONED AND ARE SHOWN AT A LARGER SCALE

CONTENTS

5 Nantucket and
Martha's Vineyard

3
Finger Lakes

2
West Virginia
Retreats

3 Suwannee
River

5
Virgin
Islands

America's
Far-Flung Hideaways

Just what makes a hideaway? That was a question we asked ourselves often as we began planning this book. To some, the word conjures images of a mountain cabin hidden away in some secluded forest. Others envision a posh resort, complete with pool, golf course, tennis courts, and gourmet restaurant. In short, a hideaway is largely a state of mind—a fact that we kept in mind as we selected the areas to be included here.

Probably no two American locales evoke thoughts of hidden getaways more so than Hawaii and Alaska—states as different as they are distant from one another. Both contain a wealth of places to slip away from it all, ranging from the rustic to the luxurious. Much of Hawaii's magic lies in the appeal of its sumptuous oceanside resorts. In Hawaii, those winter dreams of lolling in the sun in your own slice of paradise can come true, as the photographs in this introduction make clear.

Alaska, on the other hand, offers a grandeur that challenges the visitor. Range upon range of snowy mountains...a rugged, island-strewn coast ...tumbling rivers...windswept tundra—together these create one of the world's great wilderness domains. Some visitors choose to experience Alaska by staying at remote, fly-in hunting or fishing lodges. The photographs presented on pages 14-17 reveal a few of the exciting outdoor opportunities such hideaways provide.

In the four chapters of this book, we offer a range of distinctive vacation getaways. Some are hideaways in the physical sense—a real determination is required simply to reach them. Others, more easily accessible, qualify as hideaways only if you choose the right season to visit. Martha's Vineyard, for example, is a popular, often crowded, summer vacation destination. Visit there after Labor Day, however, and you experience a tranquil world usually reserved for full-time residents.

Choosing your hideaway, and picking the best time to go there, is only half the fun. It's what you do after you arrive that makes a getaway memorable. *America's Great Hideaways* offers something for nearly everyone. The adventurous can take part in a packhorse trip high in the breathtaking Canadian Rockies, or explore the demanding desert terrain of Baja California. Those whose tastes run to less strenuous activities can go inn-hopping amid New York's serene Finger Lakes, or enjoy a chartered sailboat cruise in the lush Virgin Islands.

In all, we visit 14 areas in this book. Selecting the places we covered was easy—but also a bit exasperating. It was easy because the United States, Canada, and Mexico offer so many idyllic getaways. Yet that very abundance made the choosing difficult. Some of the best hideaways had to be left out. It is for this reason that we offer this volume as a sampler of American hideaways. Every reader no doubt knows places with charms equal to those of the sites included here. If you care to, let us know of your favorite spots. Perhaps in a future book we can include them, too.

Stepping-stones to solitude, lava chunks lie scattered along the beach on the Hawaiian Island of Kauai, one of America's many scenic, far-flung hideaways. In the distance, wading fishermen try their luck in the shallow fringes of Hanalei Bay.

Free for wandering and reflection, Kauai's Lumahai Beach—regarded as one of the most beautiful in the islands—wraps a stroller in quietude. Visitors at the Sheraton Princeville (above) watch Joe Maize create a sand-coated sculpture for the hotel. Below, Craig Rogers and his wife, Brenda, ready their surfboards for a ride in Hanalei Bay.

PAGES 10-11: With the erosion-carved Waialeale Mountains for a backdrop, lush Princeville Makai Golf Course edges precipitous lava cliffs above Hanalei Bay. The resort complex spreads over 11,000 acres of a former sugarcane plantation.

Dwarfed by the splendors of the Alaskan wilds, Van Valin's Lodge (opposite, foreground) sits all but hidden among spruce foresting an island in Lake Clark on the Alaska Peninsula. Together with an adjacent preserve, Lake Clark National Park offers a four-million-acre paradise to sportsmen. Fishermen at Van Valin's Lodge can fly to any of dozens of unspoiled streams. Above, Dr. James Curtis of East Holden, Maine, plays a grayling in the Chilikadrotna River; Dr. Michael Manning (left) of Tucson, Arizona, admires a rainbow trout before releasing it in the Alagnak River.

PAGES 14-15: *Skimming a reflection of the Chigmit Mountains, a floatplane taxis across Lake Clark near Van Valin's Lodge. Guests of the resort, accessible only by air, receive an unforgettable introduction to this rustic hideaway: a bush-plane flight through glacier-clad mountain passes.*

17

MOUNTAINS AND VALLEYS:

RARE WORLDS OF GRANDEUR

By Jennifer C. Urquhart

Canada's
Rugged Rockies

T he candle wax is soft, the wick warm, as if the light seen glowing in the window had just been snuffed before the door to the cabin creaked open. But always, the story goes, there is no one there. Halfway Hut is haunted, it is said, by a skier swept away decades ago in an avalanche. With mountain guide Bernie Schiesser and some friends, I had stopped at the little log cabin on the trail from Lake Louise to Skoki Valley in Banff National Park.

On this bright summer day, we sprawled on the grass, munching sandwiches while Bernie told the story. Giants of the Slate Range, bearing names like Redoubt, Brachiopod, and Fossil, loomed gray-tan around us. More than once in my sojourn in the Canadian Rockies I would hear tales like Bernie's—stories of those who lost in the struggle against the harsh elements here, whose spirits wander ever restless in this vast, impersonal, starkly beautiful terrain.

By their very inaccessibility, mountains and valleys in places like Banff provide a special kind of hideaway. For such places often remain less touched by man. "There's a sort of energy here," said Bernie. "It almost charges the air—it comes from the love of the mountains. The longer you are here the more you sense it." For most of his 47 years the lean mountaineer has not strayed far from his mountain peaks and valleys. "I feel naked on the prairie. Mountains are like friends surrounding you." For two decades he has guided climbers and other visitors in western Alberta. From Bernie, and others here, I would gain an appreciation for the magic of these mountains, and, yes, even for their ghosts.

The afternoon was rapidly turning chill and gray. In this region, winter's icy fingers are never farther than the nearest shadow, ready always to snatch the warmth of a summer's day. We hiked through the jumble of huge limestone and quartzite blocks called Boulder Pass. Ahead of us were subalpine meadow and tundra. Bernie had to head back to town. We made camp below Hidden Lake. A gusting wind blasted us as we struggled with the tents. Dwarf willows and other slow-growing tundra plants here must hug the ground to survive extremes of cold and lashing wind. Stunted subalpine firs form krummholz— twisted clumps of trees—that grow low, with branches flagged out on one side, stripped nearly clean on the other by wind and snow. Unlike such tenacious plants, we had only to secure our tents against the wind for a single night—and to find a sheltered corner where we could light the stove to cook supper.

High subalpine areas in Banff are prime grizzly territory. Park wardens, we learned earlier, had spotted several in this particular vicinity. And we saw fresh droppings near the trail and places where ol' bruin had been digging for roots or small rodents. After dinner we carefully stashed the rest of our food many yards from the tents. But no bears came to call in the night, as far as we knew.

Pelting rain on the tent walls woke us in the morning. It took the promise of hot coffee to lure me from my snug down sleeping bag into the cold. Later in the morning the rain subsided and the sky lightened a little as we circled

*Photographs by
George F. Mobley*

*Main street meets wilderness in the peak-girt town of Banff, gateway to Canada's oldest
national park, established in 1885. In the Canadian Rockies, hideaways range from
remote campsites to world-class resorts—all set amid superlative mountain scenery.
PAGES 18-19: Limestone cliffs jut from Banff's Mount Wilson, along the Icefields Parkway.*

Ptarmigan Lake and headed to Baker Lake. A couple of mountain goats, tiny white dots on a ledge, gave scale to the immensity of this mountain world. On a more intimate measure, tiny blue forget-me-nots peeked from a rocky crevice. White puffs of cotton grass near the lake beat time to the rhythm of the wind. Beyond, in the distance, squally snowstorms veiled high valleys, sending gusts that chased us down the trail back to the car and to town.

The story of Banff National Park begins not with these snow-and-ice-capped peaks, but with a railroad, and with hot springs accidentally found in a cave in 1883 by three railroad workers. A rather small and dark cave it was, too, though one of the discoverers waxed poetic in later years about the "beautiful, glistening stalactites . . . like some fantastic tale of the Arabian nights." In the intervening 100 years this, Canada's first national park, has grown from a tiny ten-square-mile reserve set aside to protect these springs to 2,600 square miles of mountain wonderland. And Banff forms only a part of the nearly 8,000 square miles encompassed in four adjacent Rocky Mountain national parks, which include Jasper, Yoho, and Kootenay.

In the early 19th century, the Rockies were considered a nuisance, a formidable barrier to the goal of economic expansion. But, by 1880, when the Canadian Pacific Railway was pushing track across the continent, the value of such scenery and thermal waters was well known. Forceful, portly general manager William Cornelius Van Horne intended to use both to recoup his railroad's investment. "We can't export the scenery," he is said to have blustered, so "we'll import the tourists." Luxury hotels he promised to rival any in North America. What had been merely CPR Siding 29 in the Bow River Valley became the town and resort of Banff.

Heading west from Calgary a few days earlier, I had caught my first glimpse of the mountains soaring out of the prairie of southern Alberta like a ghostly, snow-covered mirage. The vision of the turrets and towers of the Banff Springs Hotel hovering above tall pines and spruces, flanked by hulking mountains, is no less startling. The spirits that haunt these baronial halls are no specters of those who found untimely death in the snows. These are ghosts of another time, an extravagant era before the First World War when, in the words of one historian, "steamer trunks . . . arrived like herds of buffalo," and dukes and duchesses might fill 22 rooms with their party and take another ten to house the servants. Today's guests are more apt to arrive by car or bus than by train and horse-drawn tallyho. And the bustle in the stylishly decorated lobbies is likely to be of the conventioneers and Japanese and European tour groups that now fill the hotel's more than 500 rooms. But the hotel remains as grand and the golf course, swimming pools, and other facilities as inviting as ever.

Set snug in the broad valley of the Bow River against a movie-set-perfect backdrop of Cascade Mountain and Mount Rundle, the town of Banff has today a year-round population of nearly 6,000, a sizable community for the Rockies. Pubs, hotels, and shops line Banff Avenue. The venerable Hudson's Bay Company store presides over all. What would the observer have thought who bewailed Banff's "overdevelopment" in 1895: "Though it consists of but a single street, it is horribly over-civilised. It has even a chemist, from whom . . . you could buy Kipling's books in the unauthorised editions. . . ." These days in Banff there is little wildlife to be found, aside from a few nightspots like the King Eddie tavern, and street names like Muskrat, Marmot, Beaver, and Wolf. But one resident did tell me about three elk that bedded down for the winter in his small yard: "Ate all the shrubs—didn't eat the hay I put out—slept on it!"

About 20 miles northwest of Banff, the Canadian Pacific's other grand hotel in the park, Chateau Lake Louise, edges a jewel of a lake that poet Rupert Brooke half a century ago characterized as "Beauty herself, as nearly visible to mortal eyes as she may ever be." Even on an overcast morning the lake was a brilliant green-blue. I followed a steep trail that led to Lake Agnes, high above in a hanging valley. The trail cut through spruce and fir forest. Dwarf huckleberries, blueberries, and delicate pink twinflowers made a garden of the mossy mountainside. Moist air exuded a pungent scent. Hikers of all ages trudged upward. Older couples paused breathless, to enjoy a glimpse of the lake below. Children darted ahead, but not fast enough to catch ground squirrels scolding from their rocky retreats. At last I bridged a waterfall spilling out of Lake Agnes and reached a small log teahouse perched on a cliff. Soon I was downing homemade soup and fresh-baked bread. Here the ground squirrels have taken up begging. "Finally," exulted a visitor from California in the guest book that day. "Beats taking the subway any day," jotted a New Yorker, by way of reply.

The Banff region inspired many of its early visitors to high adventure: exploring hidden valleys, scaling peaks for the first time, without any of the equipment modern climbers take for granted. But none matches for drollness the trip of Susan Agnes Macdonald, wife of Canada's first prime minister. In 1886 Lady Macdonald perched herself on the cowcatcher of a 60-ton locomotive to ride from Lake Louise across the Great Divide into British Columbia. She later described the fun "of this mad ride in glorious sunshine and intoxicating air, with magnificent mountains before and around me, their lofty peaks smiling down on us, and never a frown on their grand faces!"

Compared with Lady Macdonald's famous ride, my trip over the Continental Divide had the ease of a flying carpet. Banff and Lake Louise may be awhirl with crowds and activity but real getaways are only as far away as the end of a gondola ride, or a canoe trip across a lake, or a walk along one of hundreds of trails, or a helicopter lift to some lodge tucked high in a hidden valley. Jim Davies gave the controls of his chopper a gentle nudge. We rose with a whoosh. Jim was making one of his twice-weekly runs to take guests from Canmore just outside the park to Mount Assiniboine Lodge in nearby Assiniboine Provincial Park. A native of Banff and an experienced pilot, Jim knows every cranny of the region. He named lakes, rivers, little valleys, hanging glaciers as we flew over.

The chopper climbed to 9,000 feet, then 9,500. It seemed we would hit the jagged ridge that marks the Divide. Then with one last push we angled over into British Columbia. Beyond towered the massive triangular north face of 11,870-foot Mount Assiniboine. We spotted the red roof of the lodge, then quickly touched down. Sepp and Barb Renner were waiting. So were tea and homemade cakes in the living room of the old log building. But we lingered for a while in the hot sun outside, chatting with Sepp and Barb, who for the past couple of years have operated Assiniboine. Cozy little rooms in the main building can accommodate ten guests. Several small cabins house others. Next to the lodge stands the old wranglers' cabin—the "Mighty Fine Gentlemen's Club"— from the days when large packhorse groups came in. Now most people hike, bike, or, in winter, ski over the mountain passes. Some, like us, take a helicopter ride at least one way. A Swiss-Canadian, and a certified mountain and ski guide, Sepp thinks helicopters are a good thing. "We don't go to Europe on steamships any more." Barb adds, "Helicopters make wilderness more accessible for a lot of people—all ages, older, even in wheelchairs."

No matter how you get there, Assiniboine offers enough alpine charm that I half expected Barb—who looks not unlike Julie Andrews—to burst into a song from *The Sound of Music*. I wondered, too, when I saw the grizzled beard and teasing bright eyes of Ken Jones, if I hadn't found Heidi's grandfather.

"Old Grey Beard, my kids call me," said Ken by way of introduction. I followed his striding steps across an alpine meadow. Now 75, Ken has worked in this region off and on since the thirties, as mountain guide and warden. Retired now, he leads groups from the lodge on nature hikes. "Next time, you're going to get a real workout," Ken jokingly threatened Karen Moore, a visitor from Texas. We marched briskly toward the high knoll called the Nublet. "Put your feet flat going uphill," he explained. "You won't tire so easy." Ken talked of his seven years as warden. He often had to look out for ill-prepared hikers. "People don't realize what can happen in here—along this Great Divide. There's turbulence here, when there's none anywhere else. It's where winds from the north and east meet the winds from the west. Stormy weather comes in quickly."

We moved upward through spruce and fir to Lyall larches, which only grow at higher elevations. One of the few conifers that sheds its needles, the trees were beginning to turn bright gold. Needles, soft to the touch, brushed gently against my face. "They're very slow growing," said Ken. "That one is between 600 and 700 years old," he said, pointing to a foot-thick tree.

Then we were out of the trees, climbing over a steep, rocky area. On top of the Nublet grew low, compact plants: heathers, moss campions, mountain avens, arctic roses. From here we could look in nearly every direction. Little valleys below revealed small, blue-green lakes that bore names like Cerulean, Sunburst, and Elizabeth. Sometimes we heard a sharp crack from across the valley, then the roar of falling ice and rock. "People keep coming back here year after year," said Ken as we returned to the lodge. "They get hooked on the mountains."

This landscape is still changing, constantly being transformed by water, wind, and ice. Especially ice. I flew again with Jim Davies, this time toward the northern end of Banff park. From the air we could see the yawning U-shaped valley of the Bow River ground out over the millennia by massive flows of ice, and the braided channels of the North Saskatchewan River. From the air it is clear, too, that Lake Louise is only the best known of scores of beautiful lakes, also gifts of the Ice Age. In every shade of blue and green, they lie captured in high glacier-gouged cirques, or along rivers choked by glacial debris.

We reached the Columbia Icefield, its white expanse almost blinding in the bright sun. This reservoir of ice, 130 square miles in area and a thousand feet deep, straddles the Continental Divide, its waters flowing to three oceans. We climbed at times to 12,000 feet to clear ridges and peaks. The ice mass, stretching to the horizon in every direction, gives an inkling of what these valleys must have been like when they were filled rim to rim with glaciers. Then only a few of the highest peaks emerged, like small islands in a sea of snow and ice.

"Have your bones started to 'form' yet?" June Robinson asked. Not yet. And I wasn't at all sure I would ever walk again, much less fit comfortably on Rawhide's broad buckskin back. "It usually takes about three days," June promised, "to form to the shape of a horse." I would cling to that hope as well as to the high pommel of my saddle. Before there were trains, or helicopters, or automobiles, horses provided the only transport in these mountains. They still offer one of the best ways to get to remote areas. I had joined eight other riders for a 70-mile circuit through the Cascade Mountain region of the park. June Robinson and her husband, Keith, were the guides for the six-day pack trip. In winter they run cattle on their southern Alberta ranch. But in summer, for the past few years, they have herded dudes instead of steers.

Our horses lurched over rocks and boulders in the clear, rushing Cascade River, and clop-clopped across a bridge over Stony Creek to the night's camp. We took our pick of capacious yellow canvas tents in a wide meadow, but it wasn't long before everyone gathered in the cook tent, the real heart of camp, a large, sapling-framed structure. We found places at two long tables warmed between a potbellied stove and a wood-burning range. We hardly deserved the feast provided by cook Jodi McEwan: fried chicken, mashed potatoes, slaw, apple upside-down cake. It was the horses, after all, that had done all the work.

Each morning we started out about 10 o'clock for the day's ride. The horses were fresh then, and so were we. Morning light etched crenulated rock faces and high ridges and spangly aspen leaves tinged with gold. We followed trails along rivers, crossed avalanche-scoured slopes where we looked down hundreds of feet to weathered tree trunks scattered like toothpicks. We cut through dense forest, sometimes flushing spruce grouse from low branches. We rode up broad valleys. Occasionally we saw elk grazing high above us. Once we saw a young grizzly, oblivious of us we thought, loping across a far slope. At lunch we would stop in some pleasant clearing and build a fire for coffee.

On the fourth morning, when our little group headed to Cuthead Lake for a day ride, we seemed to go straight up the side of the mountain. I couldn't believe that the horses could make it. By now I trusted Rawhide's four experienced feet. She picked her way along goat trails, across near-vertical talus slopes. We reached a high saddle at about 7,500 feet, above the last vegetation in the alpine zone. Five hundred feet below us on the other side of the ridge lay the lake. Elk browsed in silhouette on the ridge above. Closer to us was a band of mountain sheep. A cold wind swept down the ridge. It was a special, awesome place. We paused, all quiet, feeling tiny against the sky and the empty rock expanse. "I'd like you to know that some of you may never get this close to heaven again," said Keith, "so take a good, long look!"

Grande dame of good living, the venerable Banff Springs Hotel (above) presides over golfers approaching a hole on the resort's mile-high championship course. Tennis, hiking, skiing, and many other seasonal activities at or near the resort challenge energetic visitors. For some, simply relaxing over lunch on one of the hotel's sun-drenched terraces (opposite) suffices. Shine or snow, the Upper Hot Springs Pool (below) remains open, pungent with sulfurous water. Banff's thermal features hold historical significance: In 1883, the discovery of nearby Cave and Basin springs by workers on the Canadian Pacific Railway led to the creation of the national park.

Gripping adventure of bouldering challenges
Barry Blanchard of the Yamnuska Mountain School
on a ropeless practice climb of quartzite cliffs near
Banff's Lake Louise. For intrepid pros and
nervous novices alike, the Banff area abounds in
opportunities to learn or perfect a variety of high-
country skills. In its namesake provincial park,
snow-clad Mount Assiniboine (above), a favorite
with mountaineers, rises beyond guide Ken Jones,
author Jenny Urquhart, center, and friend Karen
Moore as they traverse gentler slopes above
Sunburst and Cerulean Lakes. At right, Karen
and Ken, a retired ranger, enjoy a heathery resting
place well above tree line. Says Ken of the many
visitors who return year after year: "They get
hooked on the mountains." His personal romance
with the region dates back to the early 1930s.

PAGES 30-31: In a cloud of powder, champion skier
Laura Lee Bowie speeds down "Highway One," a
run in Banff's Sunshine Village. Three major ski
areas—and a season stretching from November to
June—make Banff a popular wintertime destination
for cross-country and downhill skiers, including
competitors on the World Cup circuits.

*Saddled up for a six-day outing, holiday
horse packers and guides head across verdant
subalpine slopes near Banff's Stony Creek.
Their 70-mile route will circle Cascade
Mountain. Ranging in duration from hours
to weeks, such trail rides offer a leisurely pace
and a foot-saving means of access to remote,
roadless backcountry. Glimpses of Banff's*

*abundant wildlife reward even the casual
observer. Before the fall rutting season,
a bull elk sports an imposing rack of antlers.
The golden-mantled ground squirrel at left
pauses to nibble a tender meal amid showy
summer flowers near Banff Springs Hotel.
Other animals roaming free within the park
include grizzly and black bears, bighorn sheep,
mountain goats, deer, and moose.*

*PAGES 34-35: Talus slopes of Crowfoot Mountain
sweep to Bow Lake, along the Icefields Parkway.
In the distance, the red roof of Num-Ti-Jah
Lodge lends scale to the magnificence of Banff.*

California
Gold Rush Country

Photographs by
George Herben

"We're tearing the whole mountain down, piece by piece," said Al Hauber. "Gold prospecting is a disease! I caught it a year ago. You never get over it." "You'd better grab a bucket," Jeane Stultz told me. Soon, on my knees scrunched down under a low cut in a cliff face, I set about the task of dismantling a mountain. We were at Roaring Camp, a mine near Jackson, California, in the Sierra Nevada. Jeane, who is a trim, young-looking grandmother, was almost upside down, pecking expertly with her small rock hammer. She explained "crevicing" as she dumped her diggings into a pail. "Look for flat shelves, little openings, down at bedrock. Gold will end up there." The whole system works on the principle that gold is heavier than most minerals. It will work its way down as far as it can, either into a crevice or to the bottom of a river.

When our buckets were full, we headed to the North Fork of the Mokelumne River, which cuts through this canyon. Jeane and her husband, Bob, had laid down a portable sluice, a narrow contraption with shallow compartments, between rocks in the riffling water. "The gold should get caught in the first three compartments," she said. We spilled rocks and dirt into the sluice. I grabbed at the first sparkle. "Fool's gold—pyrite," said Jeane. "Almost everybody does that on the first trip to the California Mother Lode."

We switched to panning for a while, shifting dirt and rocks in the bottom of the flat, round pans. Jeane showed me how to swirl my hand around to let worthless sand and rocks wash quickly out. "You have to get down to black sand, which is almost as heavy as gold. Then you use a little clear water to help separate any gold flecks." Suddenly there it was, a few flakes, then a tiny nugget gleaming in my pan! It does give a little thrill. And magnified by water and glass in a vial, the little nugget looked more impressive. It gave a satisfying clink against the bottom. Perhaps I was hooked!

And I had thought the gold rush was a thing of the past. Some who hammer away at mountainsides call themselves rock hounds. Dredgers comb river and creek bottoms for the placer, or alluvial, deposits. To a man—or woman—they were all hooked at Roaring Camp. A working mine most of the year, in summer Roaring Camp welcomes amateur prospectors to its snug cabins. People of many professions and all ages come here, to fish, swim, hike—but mostly to search for gold. Some, like the Stultzes, have come to Roaring Camp for many years. It was their second son, now a geologist, who gave them the gold bug, Jeane told me. "He was crazy about rocks from the time he could walk!"

"It's like the golfer's dream of a hole-in-one," Elton Rodman, owner-manager of Roaring Camp, told me. "Here you dream of a bit of gold." Elton and his partners take away much larger chunks of the mountain, using heavy machinery to gouge ore out of a gaping pit. We chatted on the porch of the camp trading post. "Whether today or a hundred years ago, this gold gets to you," said Elton. He is convinced that this little canyon on the Mokelumne is the one Bret Harte wrote about in his story "The Luck of Roaring Camp." Whether

---

Where coin-size gold nuggets once dappled shallows of the Yuba River, a latter-day hopeful tends his gas-powered dredge. In 1848, a golden glint in California's American River shaped history. Today, the Mother Lode country booms again, now with tourism.

that's so or not, the canyon is beautiful. Fig trees and live oaks stud steep, grassy slopes. Deer leap on the high ridges. At low water the river runs quietly around rocks and boulders. It is hard to imagine that during the last century men probably moved every single one of them in the frenzy to find gold.

A dozen or so people gathered at lunchtime. They compared the morning's luck, holding up little glass containers. Like old-timers in a poker game, gold prospectors underplay their success. "Didn't get one blasted piece," comments went. Or a diffident "Oh, we found our share." Al, from Florida, said "We all have jeweler's weights; it helps to have your thumb on it!"

And these people work hard—seven, eight, ten hours a day. Often the dredgers are already up at 5:30 a.m., shivering in wet suits still clammy from the day before, using vacuum-like hoses to comb through the river bottom. Joining us on the porch, one man said: "When people ask me what I did on vacation, I tell them I was moving ten-ton boulders in a river!" Do they make money? Another man answered with a laugh, "When the price of gold is good, you might be earning nine or ten cents an hour. Now, probably four cents!"

In the evening we played Scrabble by lantern light in the trading post. Most everyone drifted off to bed by nine o'clock, weary from the day's labors. It was all a far cry from the forty-niner who bemoaned his lot: "Mining among the mountains is a dog's life. A man has to make a jackass of himself packing loads over mountains that God never designed man to climb . . . ."

In early autumn, the slopes of the Sierra foothills take on a golden glow. "Think Gold," a bumper sticker ahead of me commanded. I had little chance of doing otherwise. For the region's story is inextricably tied to that elusive metal. It all started with a few flakes of gold found at Coloma, California, on January 24, 1848, in the South Fork of the American River. James W. Marshall, who never benefited from the gold he found, later wrote, "thus in a very short time we discovered that the whole country was but one bed of gold."

I was following California's Highway 49 along the western slope of the Sierra Nevada. Sometimes the road skirted low, rolling hills; sometimes it climbed high into craggy mountains. For more than 300 miles the highway links scores of gold rush towns, all that remain of perhaps 500—with names like You Bet, Humbug, Rough and Ready, Red Dog, and Hangtown—as well as countless smaller camps, which sprang up after 1848. Some are mere crossroads now, only a few shanties. Time has been kinder to others that still serve ranchers, apple and grape growers, and visitors like me. Claiming the title "Queen City of the Northern Mines," Nevada City basks in Victorian splendor. At nearby Grass Valley, the Empire Mine State Historic Park preserves one of California's largest deep-shaft gold mines. When she was a child, one woman there told me, most people were in the mines. Sometimes they "high-graded"—took a little gold for themselves. Anybody who bought something new was accused of it. She told of one ingenious miner who offered to take care of the mules: "He fed them gold—then hauled up the manure—for his garden, he said!"

Each town has its own peculiar tradition: Drytown, known for its 26 saloons; clean-cut Sutter Creek with its New England air; Murphys' tree-lined streets and charming old hotel, where such luminaries as Samuel Clemens and Horatio Alger stayed. The stories become a little grim in places like Mokelumne Hill, which had the dubious distinction of a murder each weekend for a period of 17 weeks. To the south, Columbia styles itself "Gem of the Southern Mines." Now a state historical park, the town's quiet streets mask a wild past as a city of 10,000. Fifty-five million dollars' worth of gold—at less than $20 an ounce— passed across the scales of the Wells Fargo office here. In my room at the restored City Hotel, I stretched out on the immense carved mahogany bed, long enough and grand enough that Abraham Lincoln *should* have slept in it.

Such upscale style has bypassed Volcano, a village of fewer than a hundred residents, a little off the main highway near Jackson. Here there is a comfortable patina of decay in stone ruins and an old assay office that lists a little to one side. Once 5,000 people lived here, supporting 17 hotels and three dozen saloons— and two temperance societies. It was not an easy life. Scurvy and other sickness plagued the gold-seekers. Few did more than eke out an existence. Inflation reached staggering levels. A boiled egg cost 75 cents. Onions and potatoes brought a dollar each. "It was the ones purveying to the ones looking that made the money, I've always heard," said Chuck Inman, leaning across the dark, polished wood bar of the St. George Hotel. He was right. The likes of meat-packer Philip Armour, wheelbarrow-maker John Studebaker, and small-town grocer Mark Hopkins all got their start in the Mother Lode.

"We came into town first just because of the name, Volcano," said Chuck. That was a few years ago. Now he and his wife, Marlene, own and run the vine-draped St. George. Rooms here give only a nod to modernity. The inviting old bar is usually jumping. A moose head stares blankly from the wall behind the bar. A stuffed bird perches on a shelf. Cartoons, political buttons, hats, snake-skins, and jokes decorate the place. "Everyone brings stuff," said Chuck; "they want to leave a part of themselves." His clientele is certainly kinder than were those at one early Volcano saloon. Patrons, finding the price of whiskey too high, hoisted the proprietor to the ceiling with a rope and suspended him there while they helped themselves—for free.

Volcano is not altogether a misnomer, though there's no volcano in sight. Volcanism and other geological upheavals millions of years ago thrust gold-bearing rock to the surface. Ancient rivers captured the gold. Subsequent eruptions of lava and ash buried it again until new river channels—and the hand of man—unearthed it once more.

In some areas of the Sierra Nevada, men really did take down mountains— or at least high ridges and cliffs. Gray clouds and sprinkling rain added to the somber cast of the weird moonscape I found at Malakoff Diggins State Historic Park, north of Nevada City. Spires, columns, mounds, all bleached to pale gold and pink, stretched for a mile beyond me in a barren wasteland.

After the easily obtained placer gold played out, mining operators turned to other methods to get at the metal. They worked deep-shaft mines. And in the 1850s they developed hydraulic mining. With cannon-like nozzles called monitors, the miners hurled water at such high pressure that they literally disintegrated whole cliffsides that had been ancient, gold-bearing riverbeds. Intricate systems of reservoirs and flumes supplied immense amounts of water to the sites. Malakoff, probably the largest single hydraulic operation in California, gulped more than 100 million gallons of water a day. The ecological impact of such mining was disastrous: It wasted water; and debris flowing downstream buried farms and silted rivers, causing devastating floods. In 1884, a court decision forbidding the release of such debris ended widespread use of the method.

A decade after the gold rush, it was silver—the Comstock Lode—that brought people to the eastern slope of the Sierra. Jess Machado still finds treasure in the Sierra—in its history. For half a century, he has studied the Emigrant Road followed by forty-niners and other travelers across Carson Pass. "This is one of the last parts of the road I found," he said. We stood on the most rugged stretch, looking down over boulders and rocky ledges, on a near-vertical incline. "I felt like I'd found a million dollars!" Now retired, Jess enjoys showing visitors the old trail through Carson Pass. Climbing to nearly 10,000 feet, the trail crests the highest point reached by emigrant wagons in the United States. Jess pointed out rust on the tops of rocks, where wagon-wheel rims had rubbed. "Steep pitches up and down—appalling rocks," wrote one traveler passing near here in 1849. "How will our wagons ever get through such a hell-gate?"

At its northern end, Highway 49 follows the North Fork of the Yuba River through steep canyons, then climbs high into the mountains to the little town of Sierra City. Perhaps it was the electricity going off during dinner at the Sierra Buttes Inn—the sudden quiet after the jukebox whirred to a halt, people drawing close into a circle of light delineated by a quickly lit Coleman lantern—but it didn't take long to make friends in Sierra City. And no one in town seemed to care much whether the power ever came back on. People here have more important concerns: where to meet for coffee in the morning, which stream to fish. Soon it seemed I had met a good portion of the town's population.

Gold has its lure here, too, but it may well be the glow of a sunrise along the nearby Pacific Crest Trail, or the golden tinge of a hawk's wing soaring above the 8,600-foot-high Sierra Buttes that tower behind town. In his 60s now and retired, Bob Mason grew up here. He keeps an eye on everything from a bench on the porch of the general store. "People come up here and fall in love with the place," he says. "They have good taste."

Tony Baiker of Basel, Switzerland, for one. We sat in a cafe with some local residents. Four years ago he came here for one night with his wife and small son. People in town said, "Hey, you can't leave like that." They stayed for a month. He has been back every summer since. "This country is just loaded with gold," said Tony. Has he found any? "Yes," came the unequivocal answer. Does he sell it? "Not for any money in the world. I see a speck down at the bottom of the river. I am the only person of all the billions of people in the world who sees it. It is 300 million years old. It hasn't changed a bit." But it's not only the gold. Looking around at his friends, he said, "It's knowing guys like these."

Touring the heart of gold rush country, a cyclist pedals uphill near Amador City on Highway 49. In the latter 1800s, some of the Mother Lode's deepest and richest mines flourished among these hills—and some of its wildest towns, a few still intact.

42

SCOTT RUTHERFORD

Sierra County sampler: Beneath buttes dusted in summer snow, Sardine Lake offers a cooling respite—"very medicinal to the nerves," says Sharon Miller, afloat with friend Mike Lyles. Stretching north from Highway 49, the county's chain of gem-bright lakes also lures anglers and swimmers. Glacial scouring produced most of the lakes, although one, Sand Pond, resulted as a by-product of old-time gold mining. Representing years of effort, gleaming nuggets (opposite, left) bespeak the area's still favorite activity. On the Yuba River, upstream from Downieville, first-timer Bob Ruzick tries his luck with an old gold pan purchased several years earlier at a local flea market.

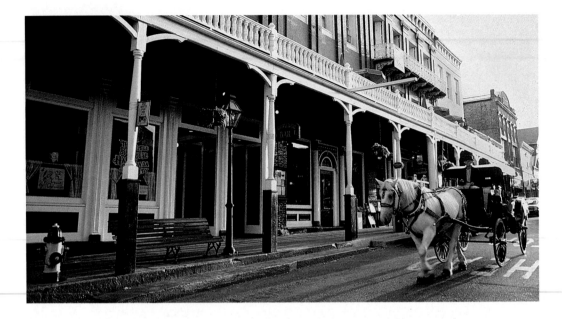

Past and present mingle in Nevada City, once "Queen City of the Northern Mines" and a place of refinement amid rough-and-tumble camps. Driver David Vertin's top hat and tails set the tone on slow-paced carriage tours. Gleaming detail of a Broad Street arcade (above) denotes the town's pride in preservation, as do its Victorian mansions of early mining and lumber barons. Below, residents Robert and Jane Butler Vaughan enjoy a meal at the National, one of the oldest hotels in continuous operation west of the Rockies.

PAGES 46-47: Solitary oak casts a circle of shade on a sere hillside near Plymouth. Tawny, tree-sparse grasslands characterize much of the dry Sierra foothills.

Appalachian Retreats
of West Virginia

Photographs by
Mike Clemmer

Hundreds of feet above us, tiny figures inched their way up the sheer rock face. "They're fools," said a gray-haired woman. "Plain crazy," her friend agreed. All eyes and two telescopes were trained on the massive, castellated outcropping called Seneca Rocks. "I saw four of 'em up there yesterday sitting on that ledge," said an elderly man.

It was a little like eavesdropping, or maybe like Tom Sawyer enjoying his own funeral. The day before, I had been one of the four on that ledge. Today, on a crisp, bright October afternoon, I could relax. At Seneca Rocks Visitor Center I watched others nearing the top of the 900-foot-high formation in West Virginia's Allegheny Mountains.

Yesterday had been different. My hands had clawed at the rock then for any crevice to grab. First I would stretch one leg upward, then out to the side, searching in vain for a niche for my foot. Then the other foot. A glance down into space. Don't look, I told myself. There seemed no way up to the little ledge where the rest of my group waited. How had they done it? "I can't," I groaned. Instructor Mike Cote, who held the rope that prevented my falling, came closer to offer encouragement. "It's there," he coaxed patiently. "You can do it."

Again and again I groped for what appeared to be nonexistent handholds and footholds, inch by inch reaching, pulling up, wedging myself into corners. My breath came short and harsh through a parched throat. Then suddenly I had made it. I crawled clumsily the last few feet over the bulging boulder and reached the ledge—and the cheering applause of my fellow climbers. Fearless Cathy Coffman, who had come here with her husband, Jamie, from Pennsylvania, bubbled with excitement. "This is *adventure!*" We had reached the first "pitch," or stopping place, of four on this route to the summit. Now there was no turning back. We were committed to the top. We continued one by one slowly climbing, belaying, and encouraging each other on the route called Old Man's.

I had joined a beginner's climbing course at Seneca Rocks in the eastern panhandle of West Virginia. Outcroppings of hard metamorphosed sandstone make this region a favored rock climbing area in the East. On the first day, Mike had instructed our class of four in belaying—handling the rope for another climber—and rappelling—descending on a rope—as well as safety procedures. "*Never,*" he repeated several times, "untie the rope attached to your harness!" There was little chance of that, I had thought.

And now we were on a narrow ledge having lunch. Our ropes were securely anchored to one of the tenacious trees that seem to grow right out of these rocks. We looked down on a hawk wafting on an updraft. The sun warmed us. "It's the ultimate escape," said 20-year-old Mike, of climbing. "You don't think of problems like cars, girlfriends, the rent." Yes, I thought, it does focus your mind. I looked up where we were headed next, a corner rising, it seemed forever, straight up toward the summit. Mike moved like a squirrel up the vertical rock slabs, placing little anchors called stoppers in crevices to hold our ropes. We

Muted lushness of eastern West Virginia's Canaan Valley gives pause to pedalers atop 4,171-foot Blackbird Knob. Though banned from wilderness areas, mountain bikes ease touring of the Mountain State's medley of rugged countryside and snug hamlets.

watched his every move, hoping for some revelation on how to get up there. Then, all at once, we *were* there, clinging to the narrow, ragged fin called South Peak. So that's why people climb mountains! There was the exhilaration of looking in every direction: down the broad green valley of the North Fork of the Potomac, and, in another direction, to steep pastures of the Germany Valley. And there was the closeness that had come with helping each other get to the top.

I sensed a closeness also among people throughout the six counties I traveled in eastern West Virginia. Perhaps it was born of the conflict that nearly rent this nation in two. West Virginia has had a turbulent history, and Harpers Ferry is a kind of gateway to that past. The view from above the little town, nestled against high cliffs where the Potomac and Shenandoah Rivers converge, is one Thomas Jefferson called "worth a voyage across the Atlantic." It was here in 1859 that abolitionist John Brown carried out his famous raid on this arms-manufacturing town. By capturing the town and its armory, he hoped to incite a rebellion of slaves. Saint or demon, Brown aroused the most intense feelings in his day, and, some say, was the spark that touched off the Civil War.

Years ago when I visited as a child, Harpers Ferry was a collection of derelict buildings. Now many of the structures have been restored as Harpers Ferry National Historical Park. And, on this day in early October, the past of this old town has come alive: It is Election Day, 1860. The region, and all of West Virginia, is still part of Virginia. Militia in homespun clothes parade on a greensward near the river. Electors orate from bunting-draped platforms on behalf of presidential candidates John Bell, John C. Breckinridge, and Stephen A. Douglas. So villainous is considered the fourth contender, Abraham Lincoln, in this region of southern sympathizers, that he does not even run here. Debaters argue heatedly over questions of slavery and the Union. "Virginia's Honor Forever Sacred!" screams one sign. Women stroll along porches of the handsome stone buildings. Some have taken up the cause of women's suffrage or of temperance. "Drunkards are found in gutters not in the polls," reads one placard.

Each year on a weekend in October, history buffs gather at Harpers Ferry as part of the National Park Service's Living History program. With great attention to authenticity of costume and dialogue, this year's 175 participants had taken on roles of that tumultuous time on the eve of the Civil War. So immersed were they in the characters they played that it was difficult for other visitors to get anyone to even speak about the present.

"You're sort of a broker between the living and the dead," said Park Service historian John King, who works with the program. "Everybody's heard the name Harpers Ferry, but they don't recall what happened here, why it's famous. We have to explain quite a bit." John, who is in his 30s and from Massachusetts, has a special tie to Harpers Ferry. His great-grandfather, at age 16, was here in the Civil War with the 34th Massachusetts Regiment. "It's pure coincidence that I have ended up portraying my great-grandfather's commander."

I followed John with a group of visitors to the small redbrick engine house where Brown had holed up with his followers and the hostages they had taken.

It was here that Federal troops ended the three-day raid. "What happened here?" John said. "Only a few people were killed. Yet it focused the thoughts of the country. It forced people to think about slavery. And the 1860 election showed it. Brown didn't free any slaves, but many contemporaries felt the first shot of the Civil War was really in this firehouse. And 620,000 men would die." A small, dark-haired woman flinched when John lunged forward as the bayonet-wielding Marines must have that October day when they stormed the barricaded door and ended Brown's raid. After the beginning of the war, Harpers Ferry changed hands sporadically, and it never recovered its former prosperity.

The Civil War and what led up to it are rarely far beneath the surface in this rumpled land. At McMechen House, a bed-and-breakfast inn in the town of Moorefield, a wall in the room where I slept is still emblazoned with slogans for pro-southern candidates in the 1856 election. The war is close in the military cemeteries large and small, and in carved stones like the one near the road at Baker, marking where a young Confederate soldier fell.

Tales of strife abound in Romney, which changed hands 56 times during the war. Everywhere are stories passed down through generations. At his farm near Petersburg, Bob Snyder, who is in his 70s now, told me about how his grandmother rode sidesaddle over the mountains to Winchester, Virginia. She had to take food and supplies to her husband, who was detained there during the war. And there was the story, told in Shepherdstown, of the postmaster who sent his daughter out each morning to see which side held the town.

But it was not only stories of war that I found in this part of West Virginia. I found tranquillity in mountain roads that wound through towns like Paw Paw, among valleys with names like Greenland Gap or Owl Hollow. Autumn had tinged leaves to glorious golds and reds and psychedelic orange. Farmhouses displayed arrangements of cornstalks, witches, and pumpkins. The air was laden with the sweet-tart smell of apples. Wooden crates were stacked in orchards. Ladders leaned against trees heavy with the season's red or golden crop.

"A celebrated and Fashionable Health Resort," 19th-century visitors described the town of Berkeley Springs in Morgan County, the earliest of the mineral water spas in the region. And George Washington really did stop here—he noted in his journal on March 18, 1748, "This day called to see ye fam'd Warm Springs. . . ." Now the bubbling waters are set aside as a state park, and I had enjoyed the "fam'd" springs many times.

But on one weekend in mid-October it is the apple that reigns in Berkeley Springs. With chrome gleaming and sirens shrilling, the fire engines have moved along Washington Street. Drum majors and majorettes have twirled their energetic best. In a red off-the-shoulder dress, Miss Exquisite West Virginia has swept through. Disguised as apples, nearly every child in town above the age of two has toddled or romped by. Lions, American Legionnaires, all have helped to get the annual Apple Butter Festival under way.

Now on the bandstand in the tree-shaded park, bluegrass fiddlers are sawing away. Quilts are flapping on lines in the breeze. Magicians are swallowing flaming torches or swords. Teams are taking turns stirring huge caldrons of bubbling apple butter. And nearly everyone seems to be eating apples in every possible form. I munched on a still-warm apple fritter dusted with powdered sugar. "I think it's a real magic place here," one woman said to me.

There is a magic throughout this region, in its history and in its natural beauty. It shows in the pride people take in showing off their world. With canoe outfitter John Zimmerer of Petersburg, I crept along a rutted dirt road into a remote valley in a four-wheel-drive van. "This is just taking us closer to heaven," he said as we jolted along. John and I canoed through the Trough of the South Branch of the Potomac River. Our boat screeched over rocks on the bottom. John paddled stern, ignoring my ineptness in the bow. I was apparently not the first to scrape the riverbed. Streaks of red, blue, and green colored many rocks. Kingfishers flashed by near the riverbank. Three great blue herons flapped heavily away at our approach. High above, their heads and tails invisible against a pale sky, two bald eagles soared unconcerned.

On another day, John's wife, Arvella, took me to the old Lyon Mill at nearby Williamsport. She grew up in an isolated hollow in Grant County. "I remember coming here with my dad when I was a kid," she said, "to get the corn and buckwheat ground." A few years ago, Jim Spicer bought the old mill, which had stopped operating in 1966. As a kind of hobby he has put it back into working order. He released water from a flume. It poured over the 24-foot-diameter wheel, causing it to groan slowly into action. Soon other smaller wheels and belts clacked and whirred away throughout the mill.

"When I first came here a sign was stuck in the old typewriter in the office," Jim said. "On one side it said 'Going Fishing,' and on the other side 'Funeral'— those were the only two excuses a miller could have for not being here." In the old days a mill was the commercial hub in remote valleys like these. Arvella and I each had bags of Lyon Mill cornmeal and buckwheat flour when we left.

There is a specialness here, too, in the warmth of the welcome I found in this part of the world—at Valley View Farm, for instance, near Mathias in Hardy County. On the porch of the little frame farmhouse, I kicked mud off my shoes. Chilled to the bone, I went inside. Some friends and I had been caught in a cold rain while bicycling in nearby Lost River State Park. Our soaked shoes were soon steaming by a potbellied stove fired up in the kitchen. The smell of fresh-baked rolls and panfried chicken only aggravated our hunger. We crowded around a table covered with bowls and platters heaped with food. We could barely move after the strawberry shortcake.

For nearly 20 years, Edna and Ernest Shipe have taken in guests at their farm. They welcome them like family in this small bungalow where they reared their own five children. Visitors come back year after year. Most of the food is produced right here. Before dinner Ernest had tromped in from the barn with a bucket of steaming milk. In the cellar, shelf after shelf bowed under the weight of mason jars of beans, corn, potatoes, tomatoes, pickles, fruit, juices. When I left in the morning, Edna gave me a big hug—and pressed a bag of fresh chocolate chip cookies into my hand. I knew I, too, would be back.

Her family heritage preserved in the painting she cradles, Edna Mott of Antioch sits before the scant remains of the Civil War-era house that once sheltered her grandmother and father. Throughout the state, reminders linger of the conflict that rent the nation.

"Our motto is 'your home away from home,' " say Edna and Ernest Shipe (left), who offer a taste of rural living at Valley View Farm near Mathias. Since the 1960s, their guests have kept returning, to hear cocks crow at dawn, to meander down country lanes, or to dawdle all day at the kitchen table. Urbanites in search of country sojourns find a variety of hostelries throughout the area. In Moorefield, proprietor Evelyn Valotto (opposite) snips geraniums for antique-filled rooms at McMechen House Inn, dating back to 1853. At Cabin Lodge in Aurora (above), once a tavern, Donald and Linda Cook unwind at fireside.

PAGES 56-57: Companionable duo, Clarence "Bill" McKenzie and Bi relax while grouse hunting in the Dolly Sods area of Monongahela National Forest. The rugged West Virginia backcountry lures hunters, fishermen, campers, and hikers.

Much of West Virginia's eastern gateway region remains enfolded in timelessness: Appalachian farmscapes cradle tiny Eglon (below), founded before 1800 near the Maryland border. In Franklin (opposite, left), fanciful Queen Anne-style woodwork frames the view of a leafy maple from a home listed, along with more than 130 other town buildings, on the National Register of Historic Places. Black-eyed Susans (opposite, right) search for the sun through a picket fence in placid Shepherdstown, one of the towns that in 1790 sought to become the site of the new nation's capital.

Place: Harpers Ferry. Time: Election Day, 1860. Quartermaster Sgt. Gartner Miller, U.S. Army Corps of Artillery, proudly passes muster in the town's annual re-creation of a fateful time. In 1859, abolitionist John Brown's raid brought Harpers Ferry onto the stage of national events, kindling passions that would steer the states toward civil war in 1861. Keeping the past alive in a different way, banjo students pick a lively tune at the Augusta Heritage Arts Workshop, a series of classes aimed at preserving traditional Appalachian arts and crafts. Held on the hilltop campus of Davis and Elkins College, the annual workshop attracts participants from all over the United States.

PAGES 62-63: Headlamps highlight a wonderland of calcite columns and stalactites in Nut Cave, near Franklin, for Rick Backus, right, and fellow spelunkers. The crumpling of limestone within ancient hillsides, which began some 70 million years ago, has created hundreds of caverns in the area; spelunkers still delight in discovering new ones.

MATT BRADLEY

LAKES AND RIVERS:

SERENE AND SCENIC HAVENS

By Erik Larson

The South's Meandering Suwannee

Photographs by
Matt Bradley

Had Stephen Foster been a stickler for spelling, things might have been very different for the Suwannee River. In 1851, the composer of such classic songs as "Oh! Susanna" and "Beautiful Dreamer" was stymied. He was writing "Old Folks at Home" and had it pretty much the way he wanted it, except for the river in the first line. Foster had chosen a river in the Carolinas, but "way down upon the Pee Dee River" lacked something. He needed another southern river. It did not matter which one, as long as the river had two syllables and sounded good. He and his brother pored over an atlas and spotted the Suwannee, a river that runs to the Gulf from Georgia through northern Florida.

It was a perfect fit, provided you whittled away a few letters and one syllable. Foster crossed out Pee Dee and wrote in "Swanee." The song was a hit, and the Suwannee became a symbol of America's South. But Stephen Foster never even saw the river.

"Well, is that important?" asked Barbara Beauchamp, a Florida folklore specialist. She was sitting on a log at the Stephen Foster State Folk Culture Center adjacent to the river in White Springs, about 30 miles below the Georgia border. Nearby, in the center's 200-foot bell tower, an electronic carillon played some of Foster's songs. "I don't think it is," she said. "The important thing is he made the river known. He broke the language barrier. Any country in the world, they sing 'Swanee River.' You test it anytime."

But can anyone spot it on the map, or spell it, or, for that matter, pronounce it? The Suwannee—you use all three syllables—gets its start in the Okefenokee Swamp in southeast Georgia, where tannic acid from decaying vegetation stains the clear water black, like strong tea. These waters tumble over a spillway into the Suwannee, then meander south through more swampland. Soon, however, the banks harden into limestone bluffs, and hardwood forests rise on either side. At White Springs, in Florida, the river turns west then follows a horseshoe path to Branford, 80 miles downstream, where the river straightens and once again turns south. Over its last 110 miles, the Suwannee broadens to its maximum width of nearly a thousand feet. Its banks sink almost to water level, and marshes replace the forests. Legend holds there is pirate treasure still sunk in the muck at Fowler Bluff, just upriver from Hog Island where the river splits in two and empties into the Gulf of Mexico, completing its 240-mile journey from the Okefenokee spillway.

For all its fame, the river remains an unspoiled waterway. The waters are clean and unpolluted. Along much of the Suwannee's path through Florida, dozens of glass-clear springs pour out millions of gallons of fresh water a day, jabbing the river's blackness with blue-green prongs. These springs are so clear you can stand on land and watch fish feeding 20 feet below the surface. Many Suwannee springs serve as doorways to underwater caves and caverns that draw divers from around the world—and trap a few each year. Less daring visitors

Cruising placid waters, a houseboat trails its spreading wake on northern Florida's Suwannee, an unspoiled river winding from Georgia to the Gulf. Beside, on, or under the water, thousands respond to the lure of meandering river or sparkling lake.
PAGES 64-65: Fishermen on Florida's Santa Fe River cast lures near gnarled cypresses.

swim, tube, and snorkel the springs. Or they fish the Suwannee and its tributaries, camp in the area's many state parks, or hike the Florida Trail where it tracks the Suwannee from White Springs to Ellaville, about 35 miles downstream.

"It's the river everybody knows, but not many've ever seen," said Dave Pierce, who moved to White Springs in 1981 to realize a dream of working outdoors, and to escape the pressures of his former job as a nursing supervisor. He guides canoe and bicycle tours on and around the Suwannee, from White Springs to the Gulf.

One Saturday in November, Dave and I and two other canoeists set out on a six-hour trip down the Suwannee, from White Springs to Suwannee Springs 12 miles away. The springs at both these towns gush sulfur-laden water, unlike most of the river's springs. "White Springs was considered to be a magical place, a neutral zone for the Indians," Dave said, after we pushed away from the bank. "Wounded warriors could come and recuperate—it was against the religion to attack them." By 1900, White Springs had become a popular spa, and in summer its population, then about 700, would double with long-term guests. In 1911, fire leveled half of the dozen hotels. Three bigger ones, built soon after, thrived through the sixties. Today, only passing motorists visit White Springs, the largest town on the river—with 900 people.

We paddled close to the limestone banks that wall this stretch of the river. Carved, bleached, and pitted, they looked like levees made from ancient shattered skulls. Cypress, holly, maples, cedars, and live oak stood atop the bank, all fused in the pale green of Spanish moss. We passed patches of white sand, brilliant against the dark waters. Once, we drifted under an oak that clutched a five-foot tree trunk high in its branches. A flood had carried the trunk there.

"The Suwannee is still the way that it has been for hundreds of years," Dave said. "It has never invited massive development on its banks. Too much flooding. There are no dams, no channelization, except right down at the Gulf. It's practically uncontrolled—we get a hundred-year flood about every 25 years."

For the night, Dave deposited us in Jasper, six miles due north of Suwannee Springs. He briefed us on how to get a room at the Jasper Hotel. "You look for the open doors," he said. "If no one's in the room, then it's yours." Ann E. Greer, "Miss Ann" to most, is the owner. I found her as does anyone who stays here—in her first-floor bedroom, door wide open, sitting on her bed among sections of the *Florida Times Union*, the *Wall Street Journal*, and a mystery novel. For 70 years Miss Ann played poker; she had a regular game for 40 of those. She came to Jasper and bought the hotel in 1934. "I thought I'd die if I stayed six months," she said, laughing. "I'm 92 years old, and I'm not dead yet."

The next morning, I joined a dozen bikers for a 25-mile ride from Jasper, south across the Suwannee, and back to White Springs. We set out about 8:30 and took a warm-up spin around Jasper. Outside town we headed west, then south through soft and green farmland. We passed barns, fields, pastures, country churches, and old men sitting on chairs near the roadside. I hadn't expected this, after seeing the lush forests along the Suwannee. If you added a few hills and took away the Spanish moss, this could have been southern New England, or Lancaster County, Pennsylvania. Even though Stephen Foster pretty much picked the Suwannee at random, the words of his song seemed still to apply—the Suwannee was indeed far, far away, in time as well as space.

At Okefenokee, the river's source, time has stopped altogether. Once, as a child, I read a story about the swamp and a mad scientist who worked in the gloom to bring the dead back to life. From then on, the name Okefenokee—say it slow and grumble a bit—always sounded to me like an incantation. With a combination of dread and delight, I drove to Fargo, Georgia, and the Okefenokee National Wildlife Refuge, 45 miles north of White Springs.

"Ever see so many buzzards before?" asked Doug Nuss, a biological technician with the U.S. Fish and Wildlife Service and also the main lawman in the refuge. We stood at the spillway to the Suwannee and watched as hundreds of vultures wheeled in the air. Others stood around in that tough-guy way vultures have. I avoided eye contact and tried to look healthy.

I joined Nuss on a working boat trip into the swamp, where I saw the Suwannee's birthplace, the channels and basins where its waters gather before they reach the spillway. I expected murk, blasted cypress stumps, and zombies. I found bright canoe trails that pass among healthy cypress, black gum, lily pads, and holly. Here great blue herons, white ibis, great egrets, and belted kingfishers flashed into view. I also got my first look at a wild alligator, this one a dark, glistening three-footer that slid off a log as we passed.

To Nuss, who is 36 and has worked one job or another in the swamp since he was 13, there is nothing mysterious or evil about the place. He likens it to the Garden of Eden. "This here's just about in the middle of it," he said. "I tell people this is where it all began."

Below the swamp, the Suwannee gathers other Georgia waters—the Withlacoochee and the Alapaha Rivers, which flow south into Florida and meet the Suwannee between Suwannee Springs and Ellaville. A third major tributary, the Santa Fe, begins and ends in Florida, but does a curious thing along the way—it disappears. At O'Leno State Park, some 20 miles east of Branford, the Santa Fe sinks underground and flows three miles before resurfacing and finishing its journey. It joins the Suwannee just south of Branford.

In addition to tributaries, about three dozen springs feed into the Suwannee. Many bear colorful names: Little River, Peacock Slough, Royal, Madison Blue, Fanning, Little Fanning. These deep artesian springs surge up through cracks in the hard clay layer that lies above the porous limestone of the Florida Aquifer, where water is trapped under great pressure. The Suwannee Basin alone has nine of Florida's 27 known "first magnitude" springs—those that discharge at least a hundred cubic feet of water per second. All are clear and maintain a constant temperature year-round, in most cases between 70°F and 75°F.

It isn't always easy to find these springs. Consider Troy Springs in Lafayette County (down here that's pronounced la-FAY-ette) six miles northwest of Branford. It's on private land, and to get there, you drive down a private driveway, pass through a gate to a cow pasture, cross the pasture, and then exit through another gate. The landowners keep the spring open to the public, as long as the public remembers to close the gates. Through the clear waters of

Troy Springs, I watched turtles prowl the submerged remains of the steamboat *Madison*, scuttled there by her captain in 1863 to avoid capture by Federal ships.

At Ichetucknee Springs State Park, ten miles east of Branford on U.S. 27, thousands of people wedge themselves into inner tubes on summer days and float the Ichetucknee River. Here nine springs spill out 233 million gallons of water a day and send it rushing down the river. The trip takes three hours, if you start at the north entrance and float to the last take-out point in the park. On some summer weekends, so many people come that the rangers close the north entrance by 10 a.m.

But early one day in November, I found myself alone here, gliding in my one-man canoe. Through the clear water, I watched mullet cruise sand channels carved at the bottom by the current. A great blue heron blasted from a tree a hundred yards ahead, sailed to treetop level, then banked left, out of sight. I did my best to prolong the trip, exploring the spring runs that nourish the river. At one point I tied my canoe to a wooden pier halfway down the run, rolled up my pants, and dunked my feet. All was cool, green, silent.

Some 40 miles south of Branford is Manatee Springs State Park, the southernmost spring on the Suwannee. During a nature walk here, I came across Ruth Tracy, a woman on the far side of middle age who was wearing jeans, running shoes, a blue sweater, and a pair of Sears binoculars. She had come to the park too many times to count, she told me, and was now camped here in a trailer with her husband, Clarence, a retired steel fabricator. They are homeless, in a sense, but that is how they want it. They sold their Tampa home in 1982, after their neighborhood was rezoned for commercial development. Instead of buying elsewhere, they became auto bedouins. "We're full-time Florida campers," she said. "We've got everything we need." She paused and grinned. "We *don't* have any rocking chairs!"

They move from campground to campground, building friendships with others doing the same thing, getting close to nature. Maybe too close, at times. Once she and her husband were out canoeing the 1,200-foot spring run that links the spring boil—where the water surges up from underground—to the Suwannee. "I'm in the bow. My husband's in the stern. And the bow starts to rise. My husband shouts: 'Alligator. Let's get out of here.' And we really dug in. I'll tell you we made that canoe move." But witnesses told them something much larger had risen under their boat—a manatee, one of the jowly, smiling sea cows that visit the springs and sometimes the spring boil itself.

Matt Meyer, a ranger at Manatee, told me visitors are surprised when they visit Suwannee country. They expect condos, concrete, and Disney-like attractions. Once, he said, a woman visiting Manatee could not accept the idea that nature delivered the spring's 117 million gallons of sweet water a day and asked to see the pumps. "When people come to Florida they see all the man-made attractions first," he said. "But this is the *real* Florida. This is what it's all about."

Clear waters of Little River Spring, near Branford, Florida, gush to the surface in a sandy oasis. Fed by the Florida Aquifer, many such springs pour forth millions of gallons daily. In the distance, the spring's waters mix with the tannin-stained Suwannee.

Rush of current pushes against divers exploring a cavern mouth at Ginnie Springs, near High Springs, Florida. Although potentially dangerous, cave diving has become a popular sport in the Suwannee area, where water has dissolved porous limestone, creating caves and caverns. At Ginnie Springs Resort, even divers without the rigorous training required for certification in cave diving can sample the sport. A steel grid limits access to safe areas near the cavern entrance. Opposite, a school of bream nibbles bread from the hand of a diver swimming in open water outside the cavern mouth. Sunlight streaming through the glass-clear water reflects from the dazzling white limestone sand.

Drifting past limestone outcrops on the far bank, canoeists float the Suwannee River on a lazy afternoon. With only an occasional dip of the paddle required, leisurely, silent trips allow visitors to spy wildlife such as deer, alligators, and beavers. Above, a great egret stands poised before the fluted trunk of a cypress. Perched atop a cooler, canoe passenger Suwannee Boy (right) offers a glance that seems to say, "Let's cast off." Owned by the managers of a canoe outfitting company, the English pointer logs hundreds of river miles yearly.

PAGES 76-77: Inner-tube captains pilot their craft down the spring-fed Ichetucknee River. Light green water lettuce, some floating loose, lines the banks beneath cypress, maple, and live oak. The three-mile ride toward the Santa Fe River attracts more than 3,000 tubers a day in summer months.

The Surprising Finger Lakes

Photographs by
Stephen R. Brown

As a child growing up in New York State, I heard the names of certain landmarks over and over again. The Catskills, Lake George, Niagara Falls. I felt I knew them, and with a child's contempt for things near at hand, I ignored them and looked instead beyond Hoboken to places like Yosemite, Yellowstone, the Grand Canyon. Those were the cover girls of national geography, against which all else paled.

The Finger Lakes fell into that pale category. They had, moreover, a dainty sound, like something you might serve at tea. But, until my visit one October, I had not known a few things about them: that autumn sets the lakeshores on fire; that 19 waterfalls flow in one state park alone; that here Joseph Smith founded the Mormon religion, and Elizabeth Cady Stanton helped trigger the women's rights movement; that you never, ever step out of the gondola of a hot air balloon until the pilot says to; that you're *supposed* to slurp at a wine tasting.

From the air, the lakes do resemble fingers, 11 of them. They occupy a 100-by-60-mile block of western New York between Syracuse and Rochester, from east to west: Otisco, Skaneateles, Owasco, Cayuga, Seneca, Keuka, Canandaigua, Honeoye, Canadice, Hemlock, and Conesus. Most of the lakes retain the names given them by the Iroquois, whose united tribes lived peacefully here before the arrival of Europeans. The longest lake, Cayuga, flows north 40 miles from Ithaca to Seneca Falls; the smallest, Canadice, flows only four miles.

Glacial ice dug these lakes, and dug them deep—Seneca plunges 634 feet, Cayuga, 420 feet. The ice also chiseled across the paths of creeks, and left them high and wet in hanging valleys. In finding their way down, these orphan streams became slender waterfalls and carved deep, narrow gorges. Trails now hug the rock walls of the gorges and climb through the surrounding hardwood forests. Swimmers, anglers, and water-skiers crowd the lakes in summer. Long a crossroads for east-west and north-south travel, the region fed the growth of new social movements and religions. History lives in its towns, with their handsome main streets and Greek Revival and federal period homes. Many of the homes are still residences, but others are museums and inns where guests can get a sense of what life was like in the region's past. Vineyards cover many of the lake slopes and turn a warm bronze in the fall—harvesttime—when thousands of visitors come to sample the region's wines, and festivals follow one another.

I arrived in the Finger Lakes as the fall colors peaked and the harvest neared its end. There would be no harvest, or at least not so bountiful a harvest, if not for the lakes. The "lake effect" buffers the seasonal changes in temperature and protects the grapes from frost in spring and fall. "For instance, last night we had 26 degrees here," said Art Hunt, who, with his wife, Joyce, owns Finger Lakes Wine Cellars in Branchport on Keuka Lake. "It was about 22 farther up the hill, and it may only have been 32 down by the lake."

The Reverend William Bostwick started the Finger Lakes grape and wine industry when, in 1829, he planted some grapes to make sacramental wine for

Nature trail passes behind Rainbow Falls in Glen Creek gorge, part of Watkins Glen State Park. Trickling for eons toward Seneca, one of the New York Finger Lakes, Glen Creek has cut a picturesque labyrinth through the region's layers of soft shale.

his Episcopal Church in Hammondsport, at the south end of Keuka Lake, and proved vines could survive here. The wine industry flourished until 1919, when Prohibition put the nation officially on the wagon. Following Prohibition, the industry began reviving, regaining its full vitality after 1976, when the state, seeking to spur the business and bolster falling grape sales, reduced license fees and regulations for wineries that produced 50,000 or fewer gallons of wine a year. More than 20 so-called farm wineries took advantage of the eased rules.

As in California, wine tours and tastings are a daily ritual in the Finger Lakes. At Glenora Wine Cellars on Seneca Lake, Karyl Hammond showed me the basic techniques of tasting. "The first thing you want to check for is clarity," she said, as she opened a chardonnay, a dry white wine. She told me to hold the glass by the stem to avoid clouding the glass with fingerprints. "Hold it up to the light. Next you should swirl." We swirled. "This releases some of the nose, or bouquet. Then you want to put your nose down in the glass so you can smell the wine. You can't be shy. If you want to be sophisticated about wine tasting, you've got to get right into it." The wine and I rubbed noses. "Then when you first start to sample the wine, when you take it into your mouth, take in a little air at the same time. Yes," Karyl said, "it's okay to slurp." I was good at that part.

The farm wineries are dwarfs compared with the commercial companies, such as The Taylor Wine Company in Hammondsport, the largest of the Finger Lakes wineries. Velda Clouter, a tour guide there, showed me a room crammed with three-story stainless steel tanks. Each tank can hold 99,398 gallons of wine—the total yearly output of two farm wineries. But the giants and the dwarfs coexist peacefully, with the dwarfs concentrating on higher priced premium wines.

At many points around the Finger Lakes, the forested and vine-covered slopes give way to gorges and falls. At Watkins Glen State Park, at the base of Seneca Lake, stone trails and steps rise 500 feet and travel a mile past 19 waterfalls (and behind two of them). At Taughannock Falls State Park on Cayuga's west bank, 12 miles north of Ithaca, the namesake falls plunges 215 feet.

In Robert H. Treman State Park, just south of Ithaca, early filmmakers, for whom Ithaca was then Hollywood, staged their Wild West and Alaskan adventures. I hiked the park's gorge trail, stone walks and steps that hug the face of the Enfield Creek gorge. The creek courses over 12 waterfalls within the park. As I walked, the sun broke through the clouds and lit the cliff above me, a sheer gray wall speckled with leaves that now caught the sun like dabs of yellow paint.

I became accustomed to the chattering and growling of the creek as it fell from pool to pool, the walkway following it down. Then I rounded a bend and found silence. Enfield Creek had left me for the thrill of diving 115 feet down Lucifer Falls. I could understand why directors used this first half mile of the gorge to film their climaxes and chases. A few dozen yards ahead, the trail turned into the woods. I turned back. Anything from here was anticlimax.

At the northern edge of Cayuga Lake, where the land is tamer and flatter, I stopped in at the Montezuma National Wildlife Refuge, 6,400 acres of protected marshland and forest, a haven for white-tailed deer, muskrats, ducks, and hundreds of thousands of Canada geese that migrate along the Atlantic flyway. In the visitor center, I stood next to a stuffed goose and watched Grady "Gene" Hocutt, refuge manager, talk to 30 kids, ages 8 to 11, from the gifted and talented program in their school in Skaneateles, a prosperous town at the top of Skaneateles Lake. (Say skinny-AT-uh-lis and you've got it.) These were sharp children. Gene did not waste time explaining why birds fly south, but talked instead of how extinction is tied to the destruction of an animal's habitat.

Next the kids piled into a bus for a ride through the refuge. When the bus stopped, they stormed out, gathered around Gene for a moment, then got down to the real business of refuge exploration, fanning out, moving in schools from one discovery—snails, pupae, frogs—to another.

Gene led them to a dam on the Seneca River at the eastern edge of the refuge, and into a forested portion farther west. He explained how the refuge had put up wooden nesting boxes for the wood ducks because there were so few old dead trees still around, and how one alien weed, purple loosestrife, had prospered because its natural competition didn't exist in this habitat. The kids were well read in such adult matters, but they were kids after all: One girl asked if the bus was stuck and if they would all have to live forever in the refuge.

Over the next few days I drove a great many back roads, each one a candidate for the perfect autumn drive. All too often I stopped to indulge a vice: antique hunting. In Geneva, I stopped at Hessney's Antiques. Its back room is chair heaven, with chairs stacked on the floor or hung from the walls. Just west of town I stopped at Calhoun's Books and Antiques and browsed among the shop's old books. Cheshire, a hamlet on the west side of Canandaigua Lake, has five antique shops just yards apart. One, The Emporium Antiques, occupies the town's Grange hall, built in 1898 as a lodge for the Knights of the Maccabees.

In the town of Canandaigua, at the northern tip of the lake, a single shop displays the wares of 20 dealers. John Cuddeback, who owns and runs the place, told me that the earliest Finger Lakes antiques date to the federal period, from 1780 to about 1810. I browsed his two floors of chests, cupboards, gimcracks and gewgaws, and came across Helen Crowley, lingering among the Blue Willow china, a pattern telling the story of two lovers who cannot marry. She tottered on the precipice: To buy or not to buy. "I never had any," she said, "and I just wanted to have some before I leave this world." She fell; bought three plates for $14.75 each. Holding them to her chest she said: "It's my beginning."

There is a different sort of action in Penn Yan, about 20 crow miles southeast of Cuddeback's on Keuka Lake. I went to the Hayes Auction Barn for the weekly Saturday night auction. This joint was jumping. Roughly two hundred people jammed the place, downing hot dogs and jelly doughnuts, sipping coffee, chewing the fat, occasionally bidding the buck or two that could buy anything from a saltshaker to a concrete chicken. The auctioneer sat atop a raised platform under a sign that read Bless This Mess. Old and newish furniture stood buried under plates, sheets, toys, tools, and lawn ornaments. "Hey," the auctioneer cried, "what do you give me for the big frog?" Her helper propped the plump and shiny ceramic amphibian on her table. It went for six dollars.

There are far larger antiques throughout the Finger Lakes—old homes

81

restored inside and out to their past elegance. On the east side of Seneca Lake, near Geneva, stands Rose Hill, a Greek Revival mansion built in 1839, a cross between a frame house and a Greek temple. In Canandaigua, the Sonnenberg Gardens and Mansion, on 50 well-tended acres, tell of the opulence of the Gilded Age. Only a summer home, the mansion has 40 rooms and 15 fireplaces, and once 60 gardeners tended the estate's roses and trees, even placing small hammocks under the melons so the fruit wouldn't fall and bruise.

One of the best preserved homes, the William H. Seward house, stands in Auburn, about 50 miles east of Canandaigua on U.S. Route 20. The house was occupied by Abraham Lincoln's secretary of state, the man behind "Seward's Folly," the Alaska Purchase. It remained in the family from 1816 until it became a museum, continuity that left most of Seward's furnishings and ornaments, and even much of his family's clothing, in place and intact.

Betty Lewis, curator for 30 years, showed me around. She told me that a 16-year-old carpenter named Brigham Young helped build the house. The future leader of the Mormon migration to Utah, Young was converted to Mormonism by the teachings of Joseph Smith, who published his *Book of Mormon* in 1830 in nearby Palmyra. Betty took me to Seward's North Library, a warm wood room with 5,000 books, including most of Seward's own working library, and busts of Seward and Lincoln. There she reached behind the pillows of a couch and pulled out Gore Vidal's novel *Lincoln*. She did her reading on the couch, she said, and was not troubled by the fact that Seward died on it in 1872.

In Seneca Falls, a village farther west on Rte. 20, Judy Hart administers the Women's Rights National Historical Park, which is devoted to preserving and interpreting the sites where the women's rights movement was born. The park includes the home of Elizabeth Cady Stanton, one of the movement's founders, who lived in Seneca Falls from 1847 to 1862, and the Wesleyan Methodist Chapel, site of the first Women's Rights Convention, held in 1848. I walked by the Wesleyan Chapel. I had the right address, but the sign said Seneca Falls Laundromat. The building was low, brick, pedestrian, with an east wall of mustard-colored stucco. I peeked in the front windows, and amid the dust and the cracked floor tiles I saw Milnor Triple Loader washers and a couple of giant Boise Comet driers. Before the National Park Service acquired the site, the chapel was used as a vaudeville hall, car dealership, athletic club, apartment house, and laundromat, and somewhere under those sediments of past use, the chapel still stands. "The chapel is a travesty. We all know it. It's embarrassing," Hart said. But she added that the chapel, due for extensive restoration, makes a point—that the history of women's rights has, until lately, been overlooked.

Some of the old houses of the Finger Lakes have found new life as country inns. I decided to go inn-hopping: One night, I stayed in an 1819 farmhouse, whose owner makes champagne in the basement. Another, I lived like a baron in a replica of an Italian Renaissance villa built as a private mansion, but later used as a Capuchin monastery. A third night, I listened for the ghosts of Belhurst Castle, a turreted mansion near Geneva, on Seneca Lake. It took 50 men four years to build Belhurst, said Robert J. Golden, the current owner and innkeeper. He led me through a guest room with an 18-foot ceiling and steps that climbed to a nook in one of the turrets. On the second floor a spigot dispensed white wine. Golden told me he bought the century-old castle in 1975 from the late Cornelius "Red" Dwyer, who had turned the place into a notorious speakeasy during Prohibition. Machine Gun Kelly was a regular, as were the World War II airmen from the old Sampson Naval Training Station, across the lake.

Local legend holds that a woman in white roams Belhurst's halls. "I think she's a figment of someone's imagination," Golden said. "But"—he paused— "there have been a number of things that have happened that were just unexplainable." Like the sound of a large piece of furniture crashing to the floor, or the cry of a baby. Once, he said, his son and a friend played with a Ouija board in the house. "And that winter the place went crazy," he said. There were, for example, sounds of a pool game in progress, but no one was using the pool table. "I will tell you," he said, "I would never use a Ouija board in here again."

Next I went tree-hopping. There is a long tradition of aviation in the Finger Lakes. Glenn Hammond Curtiss, born in Hammondsport in 1878, designed and flew the first successful seaplane in 1911. The Curtiss Museum in Hammondsport displays his aircraft and engines, as well as other artifacts from his era. About 25 air miles southeast is Harris Hill, a high plateau and a mecca for sailplane pilots. The Harris Hill Soaring Corporation runs a soaring school here and, for a fee, gives summer visitors rides in sleek, motorless sailplanes. The National Soaring Museum, also on the hill, displays full-size and scale-model gliders. At nearby Chemung County Airport, Schweizer Aircraft Corporation makes gliders, helicopters, and crop dusters and runs its own sailplane school.

One clear but windy afternoon, Bill Schweizer, 67-year-old chairman of the company, strapped me into the rear seat of a Schweizer glider, then took the controls. A tow plane yanked us into the air and towed us to about 3,500 feet, where Bill pulled a lever and released the tow rope. Our craft slowed suddenly, as if it had flown into a huge wad of cotton. The noise of the wind speeding by the cockpit softened. We were on our own. No engine. Yet I felt more secure than in a motorized private plane.

We soared at 60 miles an hour and, riding the wind that was deflected upward by the Harris Hill ridge, did not lose a foot of altitude. "I'm looking for a thermal now," Bill said. "I think we'll go down to the other end and try that." We moved east along the ridge toward Elmira, a town 30 miles south of Ithaca, in search of a warm column of air to lift us still higher. "It's sort of like fishing," Bill said. "You have to find the right currents." He spotted a cumulus cloud above us, a white puff with a slate gray bottom, and turned toward it. Cumulus clouds, he told me, form when pillars of warm air suddenly cool at higher altitudes. "They say you should head for the blackest part of the cloud," he said.

"There!" Bill shouted. "We got something." The rate of climb gauge showed us rising at 700 feet per minute. Bill turned the plane in circles so tight it seemed to pivot on its wingtip. "Look at that—going up 800 feet a minute. Now we're at 5,000. Isn't that something. We'll go to 6,000, then I'll let you fly it."

I hoped the glider would stay at 5,000.

"All right," Bill said. "Grab the controls." I grabbed the controls. I found it easy to hold the craft level and steady, nose down, speed at 60. But turning was like juggling three bean bags. When I used the foot pedals to bank the plane, the nose fell too low, and the speed rose. When I tried to correct this, the glider stopped turning. Bill took over and started his landing approach. In a glider, a landing is about like riding the express elevator down the Empire State Building. Bill explained he would bring the plane in high over the landing field, then descend fast—"Because we can't go around and try again." He pulled a lever that opened the glider's dive breaks, rectangular panels in the wing that cause the plane to drop quickly but without gaining much forward speed. We landed and rattled to a stop not far from the point where we had left the ground an hour before. I was an hour behind in my breathing.

There is a gentler way to fly the Finger Lakes. Early one Sunday, my wife and I set out from Geneva and drove to Manlius, a town just south of Syracuse. There we climbed into a wicker basket, along with Paul and Leslie Hine of Southbury, Connecticut, and Jim Griswold. Jim makes stained glass lamps and windows for a living, but flies a hot-air balloon for love, alone or with paying guests. He pulled a brass trigger on a propane burner overhead. A dragon's cough of yellow flame rose high into the $17,000 balloon overhead, heating its two tons of air. Within seconds the balloon was lighter than air, and we rose without a sound above the treetops. There is no way to determine exactly where a balloon will go, nor how fast it will go there. So Chip Schilling, also a balloon pilot, followed us from the ground, rattling up and down paved and unpaved roads, struggling to keep us in sight.

We drifted west, over dark black ground flecked with orange and red. We pulled leaves from the topmost branches of trees and watched as a herd of sheep stampeded to their water trough for a conference on aerial phenomena. We passed quietly over a hunter who walked a dirt road in a field, carrying arrows and a bow. He did not see what we saw—six deer bounding across a field just a few hundred yards west, and moving fast away from him. I wondered if deer knew how to snicker.

Too soon, the trip was over. We passed low over a farmhouse and hit the lawn once, tipped forward, bounced up, struck again, and continued skipping a few more yards. "Whatever you do, stay in the balloon until I tell you it's okay to get out," Jim said. Otherwise the balloon, its load suddenly lessened, would have rocketed skyward.

We came to rest in the yard of "Hunter's Paradise," a home owned by Mrs. James J. Carroll. Delighted with our visit, she invited us in for hot chocolate. When Chip arrived, we packed away the balloon and broke out the champagne. Jim offered the balloonist's prayer: "The winds have welcomed you with softness,/ The sun has greeted you with its warm hands,/ You have flown so high and so well/ That God has joined you in laughter/ And set you back gently into/ The loving arms of mother earth."

Astronaut Sally Ride, at podium, returns a scarf of Amelia Earhart's to the National Women's Hall of Fame in Seneca Falls, New York. In homage to Earhart's pioneering role in aviation, the scarf rode into space with America's first spacewoman in 1984.

Motorless whisper of sailplanes and the roar of race car engines proclaim the varied activities that draw visitors to the Finger Lakes. Warm winds sweeping from valleys to ridgetops favor soaring here, where in 1930 pilots gathered for the first national soaring contest. The sailplanes above circle near Elmira in search of thermal updrafts for lift. A wingtip-mounted camera casts the shadow in the foreground. Opposite, world-class drivers drift through an uphill S-curve at Watkins Glen International Raceway. Circuiting the 3.4-mile endurance course 92 times, drivers battle 11 turns—and each other—for 500 kilometers, before crowds of up to 70,000 spectators.

PAGES 88-89: Hot-air balloons float above Skaneateles Lake near Syracuse. "We go wherever the wind takes us," says balloonist Jim Griswold, one of 20 members of the Central New York Balloon Club. Visitors may pay to ride in the gaily colored craft.

Summer visitors at Rose Hill, a restored Greek Revival mansion on Seneca Lake,
get a glimpse of rural elegance of the 1840s. Finger Lakes shops such as Canandaigua's
Emporium Antiques (below) attract browsers and buyers; ubiquitous garage and yard
sales (above) tempt passersby with the chance of discovering an underpriced treasure.

PAGES 92-93: Glowing maples near Seneca Lake accent a vineyard of concord table grapes
ripening in the foreground. Also favored by moderate lakeside climates, other grape
species await harvesting for the region's noted wines, champagnes, and sherries.

Lake-Strewn Heartland
of Minnesota

Jim Ekstrom sat at the rear of his small outboard boat under low and gray October skies. He wore a rabbit-skin hat. He had shot the rabbit. He wore a deer-hide vest. He had shot the deer. He wore an artificial leg. He had shot the left leg, eight inches of it, clean off in a 1973 hunting accident—a mishap he shrugs off casually. Once, while waiting for a new artificial leg to replace an old one, he went hunting. ("I'd rather hunt than eat," he told me.) He leaned on his crutches, braced himself against a tree, and bagged a bear, whose pelt now lay across the bow of his boat. "Sit yourself on that bear," he said. "Keep you warm." Jim, a hunting and fishing guide, started the engine and steered us out onto Big Wolf Lake, some 200 miles north of Minneapolis, Minnesota.

The Ojibwa Indians called this territory *Minsi-sagaigon,* "everywhere lakes." To locals, it is the north woods or north country, a chunk of Minnesota between Mille Lacs Lake, 90 miles north of Minneapolis, and Lake Bemidji, another 120 miles up the road. The terrain resembles a water bed blasted with a shotgun. There are 1,300 lakes just within the Chippewa National Forest at the north end of the region. Mille Lacs is the region's largest lake, a nearly circular body of water 18 miles long by 14 wide, yet so shallow that even minor squalls can raise boat-swamping waves. The Mississippi, the nation's biggest river, gets its start in the region, flowing out of Lake Itasca as an inches-deep stream.

Paul Bunyan, the giant lumberjack of Minnesota legend, was supposedly born in this area, a symbol of the logging industry that once thrived here and opened the area to settlement. Bemidji, on the western shore of Lake Bemidji, does not let the legend go unnoticed. A dozen establishments use Paul's name, including a sandwich shop and a trailer court. He is listed in the Bemidji white pages (the number gets you Nordheim Roofing and Sheet Metal Company) and his statue, 18 feet tall, $2^1/_2$ tons, stands by the lake alongside Babe, the Blue Ox.

Today someone ought to consider building a memorial to the resort trade. Hundreds of resorts line the lakeshores. The smallest are the fishing camps, rustic collections of housekeeping cottages. The closer you get to Minneapolis, the larger and flashier the resorts, with golf courses, pools, tennis courts, and organized activities. In the Prohibition era, gangsters used to hide out and gamble among the lakes. But things have simmered down. Now families come in summer to swim, fish, hike, and canoe. Spring and fall draw couples looking for escape. Even the north woods winter doesn't scare people off. Hundreds of skiers compete each winter in Bemidji's Minnesota Finlandia 54-kilometer cross-country ski race, and in the shorter Bemidjithon held the same day.

Fishing, however, is the big attraction year-round. Anglers seek walleye, northern pike, or, when they feel like spending long hours exercising their casting arms, muskellunge or muskie, a large and crafty fish that is far less common than the other lake species. The state's record catch was a 54-pounder pulled from Lake Winnibigoshish (Big Winnie, for short) about 35 miles east of Bemidji. Few fishermen are lucky enough to land such a monster, but everyone

Photographs by
Scott Rutherford

Sliding below the horizon on the western shore of Caribou, one of more than 15,000 lakes in northern Minnesota, the setting sun ends a tranquil day for two vacationers. In this lakeland region of large and small resorts, escape comes as easily as a stroll down a pier.

seems to have a tale of some bizarre muskie encounter. One muskie supposedly leapt from the water and landed in a man's arms. Another came up and bit an angler's hand as he cleaned and rinsed his fish in the water at the shore of a lake. Mostly, though, fishermen talk of frustration and how a muskie will follow a lure all the way back to a boat, but never strike.

"As they say, it takes 10,000 casts before you catch a muskie, or even see one," said Jim Ekstrom, who caught a 38-pounder one November day and just about swamped his boat in the process. Jim and I crossed to the northeast rim of Big Wolf Lake, entered the Mississippi and used it to cross to Lake Andrusia. Jim told me he was born in 1933 in a house near Andrusia and had hunted, trapped, and fished the area since he was a boy. We passed an island that had once served as a Hudson's Bay Company trading post, and skirted plains of wild rice at the water's edge. A gourmet treat elsewhere, wild rice is a staple for the Ojibwa Indians on the Leech Lake Indian Reservation, who harvest the rice from canoes each August. The Ojibwa reservation covers 920 square miles. It includes two-thirds of the Chippewa National Forest and some of the region's biggest lakes, Leech, Cass, and Winnibigoshish.

Jim told me that fall and spring offer the best fishing in the lakes. But after two hours of walleye fishing on Andrusia, we had only one tiny walleye and three small perch. "Today sure isn't an example for fish," he laughed. "The other day I had my limit in 42 minutes. Six walleye. I threw four back, just kept the big ones, average two to three pounds." We moved onto adjacent Cass Lake and went for northerns, casting red and white lures that, when we reeled them in, spun like barber poles.

The day had turned chilly, not uncommon here in October. When snow began to fall, we fled to Jim's home, part log cabin, part frame house, on a bluff where the Mississippi meets Lake Andrusia. After a meal of fried eggs and ham, Jim showed me early 20th-century photographs of sleek speedboats, lake steamers, and Indian tepees—not the kind you see at tourist trading posts, but actual housing. Priorities changed over the years. "At the turn of the century, everybody wanted land away from the lakes and the cold, where you could raise a few crops, have a couple of cows." Jim laughed. "Now it's just the opposite. Everybody wants to be on the water."

In the Bemidji area alone there are more than 40 resorts, many of them so-called ma-and-pa outfits. I spent a few nights at one, Wolf Lake Resort, owned since 1970 by Kermit and Mary Bjerke. I stayed in a simple lakeside cottage. Mary and I canoed a portion of the Mississippi below Lake Bemidji, where the river, after traveling north a hundred river miles from Lake Itasca, widens and turns south. We glided by trees felled by beavers and past clusters of tamarack, conifers that flare a brilliant orange before losing their needles each fall. Through the clear water we could see the sandy bottom and the shells of clams.

Just beyond one bend, a large bird rose suddenly from a pile of river debris. It moved downriver, slowly pumping its huge wings, and showed us the white feathers on its head and tail. A bald eagle. It swept up above the trees and out of sight. I was elated. Yet for locals, such encounters are common. "It's almost impossible to spend a week here during the summer and not see an eagle most days," said David M. Johnson, a wildlife biologist in the Chippewa National

Forest. Based at Cass Lake some 15 miles southeast of Bemidji, Dave told me the forest has about a hundred breeding pairs of bald eagles, the second greatest number in the United States; Alaska has the most. He showed me one nest, empty this time of year, and explained that the locations of Chippewa's 200 or so nests must be kept confidential. In early spring, sightseers could flush an eagle from its nest at a critical time, and perhaps keep its eggs from hatching. Also, Dave said, "there are still people that shoot eagles."

In Walker, I met Stephen Lund, founder and executive director of Camp Fish, where kids rich and poor learn to fish. In the summer of 1985, a thousand children—and 200 adults in the parent-child programs—went through the camp. They came from 24 states and six foreign countries. "Fishing has given so many kids a chance to feel good about themselves," Stephen said. "It's a sport that doesn't discriminate physically. It doesn't discriminate financially. It doesn't discriminate intellectually—you don't have to be a Rhodes Scholar to fish."

Fishing contests are a north woods staple, but none comes close to the International Eelpout Festival, held every February. Ken Bresley, owner of the Tackle Box in downtown Walker, started the contest when, after moving here in 1978, he saw how winter numbed the life out of the town. (Leech Lake holds Minnesota's record low temperature: –59°F set on February 9, 1899.) He decided to hold an eelpout contest to parody the other contests, and spark some fun. The eelpout, a sort of cross between a snake and a catfish, is the pariah of the lakes. "Even when you do catch one, you're not going to *tell* anyone," Ken said.

The festival became the Mardi Gras, north woods style. A thousand people came to the first festival in 1979—not bad considering Walker has 970 people. In 1984, around 10,000 came, some by chartered bus from neighboring states. Participants try their best to deny that winter is winter. There is a formal dinner on the ice to which guests must wear a gown or a tux. It is permissible— and prudent—to wear it under a snowmobile suit. A team of revelers from Pine River builds a replica of their town on the ice, complete with fire hydrants and streetlights. And the festival organizers make sure the fishing conditions are as good as possible. "Eelpout bite best when the wind is blowing from the east," Bresley said. "So we put fans on the ice to make sure the wind is blowing the right direction." For lures, anything goes. Vera Kinder, who with her husband, Orville, owns Forestview Lodge on the south shore of Leech Lake, told me she turned her old dental bridge into a lure for the festival.

Forestview Lodge, which opened in 1924, is one of the mid-range resorts in cost and luxury. It is not so large as the southern complexes, but has 20 cabins (many built of logs cut from the surrounding woods), one condo, a pool, and a rustic timber lodge with a restaurant and bar, all set on 75 acres of shoreline forest. When I checked in and asked for my key, Vera, who claims people call her "the jolly little fat girl behind the desk," frowned: "Oh no. No keys at Forestview for 61 years."

The big event here comes in mid-May, with opening day of the fishing season. The Kinders open Forestview the night before and are booked solid a year in advance. "It's a special time after being closed in all winter," Vera says. "People are anxious to get out on that water."

The north country's winters are indeed bitter. Yet its cold, pure air once was regarded as a cure for tuberculosis: A former sanatorium, the *Ah-gwah-ching* (Ojibwa for out-of-doors), stands outside Walker—one of many surprises I found here. Elsewhere, remote canoe trails contrast with man-made water slides, log cabins with lakeside town houses. Acres of wilderness stand near posh golf resorts. About 15 miles south of Walker, I found an especially appealing wilderness, the Deep Portage Conservation Reserve. Thirty miles of trails cross its 6,000 acres, passing among dozens of lakes, Prussian blue in the clear fall sun. Yet just to the south are luxury resorts along Pelican and Gull Lakes.

In Brainerd's Pine Beach area, I met Sherman Kavanaugh, president of Kavanaugh's, his family's 38-unit resort on Sylvan Lake. He calls this area "the Cape Cod of Minnesota." His guests stay in cottages and "lake villas," swim in the indoor pool, play tennis and golf, dine at the resort's gourmet restaurant. "People want things nicer and nicer, and they've got the money to pay for it."

In Garrison, where State Route 18 meets Mille Lacs, a giant walleye, the concrete kind, welcomed me to town. Beyond the statue the lake frothed in the brisk autumn wind. Old wooden launches, for hire and bristling with tackle, bobbed on the waters and gave the scene the feel of a 1940s movie. As I drove beside the lake, I passed storage yards crammed with what looked like red outhouses. In winter, ice fishermen rent these houses and tow them onto the ice, building an instant city of 5,000 houses known as "Frostbite Flats." The ice even draws a crowd when it breaks up each spring, sometimes piling so high that it blocks lakeshore roads.

For the night, I checked into Izatys Lodge, a large resort on the south shore of the lake. After I registered, desk manager Ann Anderson showed me a stack of Tyrolean felt hats. "What color would you like?" she asked. I picked a red one. I looked over a sign-up list that included such things as crazy golf, fishing, and doubles tennis; there was a dance set for the next night. In the bar, a couple of dozen men and women sang and clapped as a man with skinny legs and lederhosen played "Roll Out the Barrel" on a piano. I had arrived just in time for the Oktoberfest, marking the resort's last weekend of the season.

Herb J. Carlson, whose parents took him for drives around Mille Lacs in a Model T Ford back in the 1920s, said he and his wife have come to Izatys since 1970. "You can just come up here and do what you want," he said, sitting in the bar. Outside, a launch pitched in the waves as it made its way back to the Izatys dock. "If you want to go goofy, you can do it. But if you want to just relax, why, that's fine too." Here in the heartland of Minnesota, the Carlsons have found their own way to escape, an escape to the warmth and friendship of couples they have met over the years. "You get a sense of belonging," he said. "I think that's the bottom line. A sense of belonging."

Ankle-deep in Pelican Lake, 14-year-old Cory Resler concentrates on baiting his hook. Game fish from small, hard-fighting lake trout to giant muskellunge attract fishermen to Minnesota's lakes and streams. What's Cory fishing for? "Anything that bites."

Primitive to posh, Minnesota's resorts cater to a wide range of tastes. Madden's, the state's largest resort and conference center, spreads across Pine Beach Peninsula on Gull Lake. The resort features three beaches, two marinas, 45 holes of golf—and some of the region's best walleye fishing. At one of the golf courses, William Bickford (opposite, right) waits for his grandson, Christopher Momberg, age 7. During lakeland vacations, forgetfulness often overtakes calorie-counting guests: Owners Sherman and Mae Kavanaugh (opposite) show off some of the temptations of their Brainerd resort's restaurant.

PAGES 102-103: Their everyday cares forgotten or dismissed, relaxing vacationers at Madden's Resort quietly contemplate a passing motorboat of fishermen.

Offering solitude and the solace of nature, the attractions of Minnesota's lakes reach far. Susie Cram (opposite), a senior at Sam Houston State University in Huntsville, Texas, paddles a canoe on a three-day trip with her two sisters in Chippewa National Forest. "We camped out under the stars, talked, caught up with each other's news—I hadn't vacationed with my sisters in years. It was wonderful," recalled Susie, a college rodeo athlete. Below, a camping couple unpacks at a lakeside campsite in Scenic State Park, just outside Chippewa National Forest. The popular state park contains more than 30 species of orchids, all found in an area of less than 2,000 acres.

PAGES 106-107: Sails trimmed taut on a starboard tack, racing catamarans skim sun-sparkled Gull Lake. An annual three-day regatta, sponsored by the Gull Lake Yacht Club, draws sailors from across the Midwest in late summer. From the cool springs of the South to the North's soft breezes, from competition to contemplation, hideaways tucked among America's lakes and rivers offer a wealth of pleasurable escapes.

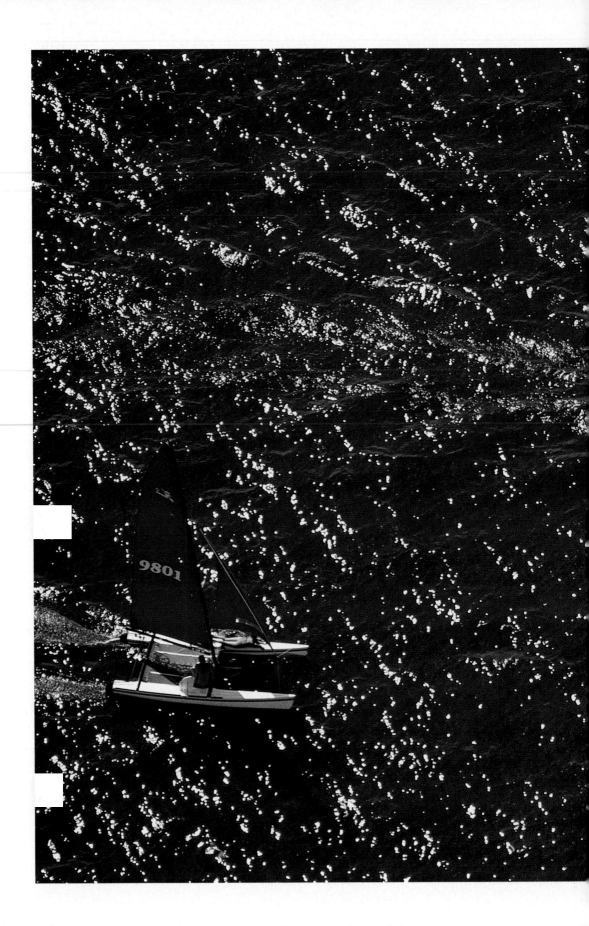

DESERTS AND PLAINS:

REALMS OF BROAD HORIZONS

By Thomas O'Neill

MIKE CLEMMER

Arizona's
Arid Historylands

*Photographs by
Mike Clemmer*

P ast a line of women supine in bikinis, past a pack of men tossing a football, past grills smoking with steaks—past all diversions—John and I hurried, bird-watchers on a mission. Everyone else was half-dressed. We wore muddy jeans and sweat-stained shirts; our arms were scratched; binoculars bounced off our chests. We turned down a path that ran alongside the blue acreage of water at Patagonia Lake State Park in the southeastern corner of Arizona. Time: 3:30 p.m., only two hours before dusk. Temperature: 85°F. Date: October 12. John had noted it all down in the truck; now we were pushing aside tree branches, slapping at mosquitoes, slopping through a marsh.

"Look!" John commanded. Glasses up. "That's a cormorant, a double-crested one," he said crisply, identifying the large, dark water bird perched on a snag in the middle of the lake. "That's number 87."

Unlike bathers, ball players, or barbecuers, I was not indulging in a relaxed Saturday afternoon. John Saba, field trip director for the Tucson Audubon Society, was instead exposing me to the rigors and revelations of a 100-Bird Day. Our task was to identify a hundred different species of birds during the daylight hours. In few areas of North America could one pull off this feat, but southeastern Arizona is undeniably one of them. A mecca for birders from around the nation, the region consists of arid grasslands with cool, pine-topped mountains rising in their midst. Here lies a meeting ground of alpine flora that extends from the Rocky Mountains in the north and more heat-resistant vegetation common to the Sierra Madre Occidental of Mexico to the south.

More than 450 species have been sighted in this corner of Arizona. The list includes such crowd pleasers as multihued tropical birds from Mexico that come for the summer—trogons, hummingbirds, and, for the first time in the United States, the flame-colored tanager, sighted in the Chiricahua Mountains in April and May of 1985. "Mountains tend to concentrate birds," John had explained to me. "Out here in the desert we call the mountains 'sky islands.' Every bird coming through looking for a nesting site or on a migration route is drawn to these well-watered and forested oases."

I knew that John was a serious birder when he asked if I owned any camouflage gear. We ended up going undisguised, but John came well equipped, nonetheless. His stock included a $600 pair of 10-power binoculars, a 20-power telescope, four field guides, and waterproof boots. "I'm a gentle fanatic," John admitted as we drove south from Tucson at daybreak, mist rising wraithlike from the ground. "If I were a real fanatic and wanted to do a big day where our goal was 200 birds, then we'd have gotten up at 2 a.m., climbed a mountain to hear some owls, and stayed out till after dark, with 20 minutes to a stop. Let's call this a relaxed big day. I want to be able to spend one to two hours at a spot."

The first habitat we visited was Canoa Pond, a muddy bed choked with chest-high reeds. Good birders often identify a bird by its call before they see it,

*Ciphers from the past, Hohokam petroglyphs, among thousands in the area, cover
a boulder in Saguaro National Monument, near Tucson. Their meaning, baffling to
explorers, pioneers, and prospectors who successively trod these arid lands, remains elusive.*
PAGES 108-109: *Weathered China Peak looms above riders in the Dragoon Mountains.*

John said, falling into something of a trance as we stationed ourselves under a nearby cottonwood and listened.

Chug-chug-chug-chug. "Cactus wren," John said quickly. "It sounds like a car trying to start." *Whit-wheet.* "Curve-billed thrasher. There it is." *Churr-churr-churr.* "Listen to that Gila woodpecker chatter." A flash of yellow was a western kingbird; a flash of red was the cardinal-like pyrrhuloxia. Long flapping wings belonged to a great blue heron, short pointed ones to a kestrel, a small falcon. And so on. At the close of two hours we had chalked up 40 species, a great start.

John tried all sorts of places. On the banks of the Santa Cruz River, we spotted lesser goldfinches, coots, and pied-billed grebes. On a lily-pad-covered pond at a cattle ranch, the rare northern jacana, a long-legged and long-toed shorebird, treated us to a glimpse of its brilliant yellow underwings. The brambly rough on the tenth hole of the Kino Springs Golf Course produced a rufous-crowned sparrow and a western wood-pewee. We even made the rounds of two sewage ponds and came up with 16 birds, mostly ducks and shorebirds.

By five o'clock, our total stood at 93. I was amazed at the profusion of bird-life and delighted by John's instructive company. Just seven more birds to go, we reminded ourselves. We pulled off a highway and admired a flock of white-throated swifts swooping about a cliff swabbed orange by the setting sun. Ninety-four. A bridled titmouse flitted near a mesquite tree. Ninety-five. Darkness began to infiltrate the sky. That's it, I thought. But outside the town of Patagonia, John spun the truck in an abrupt U-turn. "I think I saw an eagle," he exclaimed. We halted at a grove of trees and in the failing light stared at a large bird roosting on a branch. "Oh, it's just a turkey vulture," he said. "I guess we don't make our hundred." Neither of us was upset. It had been a fantastic day.

The mountains in this corner of Arizona attract more than birds. On an early autumn day, when dust devils spiraled from the alkaline flats of Willcox Playa and a tremor of heat waves blurred the valley floors of creosote bushes and straggly yucca trees, the heights of the Chiricahua Mountains presented a sense of luxuriant sanctuary. Silvery streams rushed through beds of lichen-spotted boulders; a black bear lumbered through a scented pine forest, unaware of our eyes; and on a high, breezy meadow one could lie down without fear of thorn or snake. Rearing as much as 9,800 feet above the parched plains, this sky island a hundred miles east of Tucson is something of a privileged secret among rock climbers, mountain bikers, bird-watchers, and backpackers, who migrate to its cool heights during the fiery months.

On the range's western flank I hiked a loop trail through the Chiricahua National Monument, set aside because of its forest of bizarre rock pinnacles, the remnants of an ancient, dissected lava flow. The enormous columns of weathered stone humble the Douglas fir and ponderosa pine growing among them. The landscape felt primitive and magical, as if moonglow would reveal mysterious ceremonies full of chants and dark, whirling shapes.

Apache Indians from the San Carlos reservation to the north, I learned, do regard the Chiricahua Mountains as sacred. Apaches from the Great Plains first drifted into these mountains in the 1700s, finding a stronghold where they could resist waves of colonization, first from Spaniards and later from American settlers. Traveling in small family bands, the Chiricahua Apaches, identified even from afar by their shoulder-length hair and their headbands, cherished the mountains for the food, water, and shelter they supplied.

In 1858, the Butterfield stagecoach line began crossing the range, soon followed by detachments of U.S. Army troops. In response to the encroaching white civilization, Apache raids, traditionally aimed at livestock, escalated into attacks on people. From 1861 to 1872, the redoubtable Apache chief Cochise waged war from the Chiricahua and nearby Dragoon Mountains. And it was in this locale that the name Geronimo, signifying the last great Apache warrior, struck fear in the hearts of soldiers and settlers alike.

North of the Chiricahua National Monument, in a hushed bowl of hills, lie the skeletal remains of Fort Bowie, staging area for the final offensive in the Apache conflict, and today a national historic site. Taking the 1.5-mile path to the fort, I sensed how history haunts the surroundings. A ridgeline speckled with juniper trees looked like an ideal place for an ambush. Under a bower of trees stood the site of Apache Springs, near where a company of California Volunteers withstood a furious attack by Cochise and several hundred warriors. At Fort Bowie, broken adobe walls and an overgrown parade ground recalled the anxiety and isolation of the embattled soldiers, strangers in a strange land.

"The Apaches were masters of guerrilla warfare," Bill Hoy, chief ranger at Fort Bowie, told me. "It was hit-and-run: maximum gain, minimum loss. In the case of Geronimo's band, the Army spent more than 20 years with thousands of men trying to corral a small group of hostiles. And they never really defeated them." Exhausted by their flight from military patrols, Geronimo and his band of 37 men, women, and children surrendered on September 14, 1886, at the mouth of Skeleton Canyon, southeast of the Chiricahuas. On Arizona Highway 80, near the windswept hamlet of Apache, stands a monument commemorating the historic event which, except for the Sioux outbreak in South Dakota in 1890, marked the end of the Indian wars.

History shadows one's movements all across southeastern Arizona. Most roads lead to ghost towns—Paradise, Gleeson, Pearce, Dos Cabezas, Double Adobe—where ofttimes a few hardy souls hang on. Mining booms went bust here in most cases, and nothing died faster than a played-out camp. In the mid-1970s, when its famous copper mines shut down for good, the town of Bisbee, a mile high in the Mule Mountains, appeared as if it, too, would join the deceased. But then the town discovered that not all its riches were underground.

Emerging from a tunnel through the mountains, I drove down into a steep canyon where houses cling to the hillsides like plants in a rock garden, and through a business section lined with turn-of-the-century edifices of brick and stone. Farther on gaped a huge crater, the scar left by an open-pit mine. Only ten years before, many of the houses were abandoned, and the shops boarded up. Now, astonishingly, that once decrepit place was humming with life.

People, many of them young, were congregated around the post office, sharing news and reading mail. (The precipitous streets of Bisbee's old section prohibit house-to-house mail delivery.) Tourists peered into the windows of art

113

galleries. A roll of plush red carpeting rested outside a storefront where, inside, carpenters and electricians were finishing renovations on what was to become the Bisbee Grand Hotel. On a prominent clock tower, the hands of Mickey Mouse impishly indicated the hour. Time had not jarred to a stop in Bisbee.

"It was predicted Bisbee would be a ghost town by the early 1980s," said Jean Redmond, an expatriate from Detroit and former director of the local chamber of commerce. We sat drinking coffee in the old company store, now a stylish restaurant accented with splashes of neon. "The town lost 1,600 jobs when the Phelps Dodge mines closed in 1975," she said. "The population, once near 12,000, dropped by half. By the late 1970s Bisbee was legally bankrupt."

What resurrected Bisbee—to the point that its population is growing again and its debt has been retired—was a combination of new blood and an awakening of self-sufficiency. As a first move, the town adopted a modern precept— sell thyself. Now Bisbee plays host to a national bicycling race in April. Town officials convinced the U.S. Army to shoot training films in the old district. Festivals sprang up, celebrating everything from poetry to gems and minerals. Laid-off and retired miners removed tons of debris and replaced hundreds of feet of railroad track so that the old Copper Queen mine could be opened for tours. Meanwhile, a steady stream of newcomers moved in, attracted by the picturesque location and the low prices of the former company homes.

On a bright, airy day, I walked through the stolid old commercial district— now on the National Register of Historic Places—and up Brewery Gulch, once a ragtag of saloons and brothels that, in the early 1900s, was described in a newspaper as the "hottest spot between El Paso and San Francisco." Ramshackle dwellings alternated with houses showing off new wooden doors, skylights, and wind chimes—all signs of rescue. Back on Main Street I stopped in a gallery owned by Les Johnson, a rangy, bearded fellow who could double as one of the prospectors who used to rummage in the hills. Meditative earth tones from the desert stood out in the paintings and Indian rugs that hung from his walls.

Les told me that one of his best sellers is Michael Stack, a soft-spoken red-head whom I later found at work in a former miner's cabin. In his cluttered studio, Michael was applying the last touches of oil paint to a desert landscape. The sky was magnificent, a luminous upwelling of lavender-tinted clouds. "The nice thing about working out here," Michael said, "is that if I get bored, I just get in a car with my easel and soon there they are, all these incredibly beautiful scenes."

I ended up having a crush on Bisbee. To know that a small town with the community spirit of a college campus and the diversity of an urban neighborhood really did exist was thrilling. On my last night there, I stood on a ridgeline above Bisbee with some new friends and looked down at the town. "It looks so unreal, like someone dreamed it up," I said, gazing at the twinkling of lights in the canyon. "Yes, sometimes it does seem like make-believe," came the response. "Why do you think we stay?"

Battlements of volcanic rhyolite overshadow riders in Chiricahua National Monument —11,000 acres rising from desert to cool mountain woodlands. Popular with hikers, the rugged trails of the monument thread a landscape once the haunt of Apache warriors.

Beyond rolling rangeland, Red Mountain (opposite) crowns the rumpled Patagonias less than 20 miles from the United States-Mexico border. The area's beauty has earned it renown as a setting for several films, including Oklahoma and Red River. Economically, cattle and copper long ruled eastern Arizona. Today, its abundance of sunshine makes the region ideal for guest ranching. At Patagonia's Circle Z Ranch (above), swimmers and loungers unwind in an inviting oasis. Horseback riding ranks as the favored activity at most such establishments, whether working or dude ranches. On an overnight pack trip, guests of Grapevine Canyon Ranch (left) camp beneath Emory oaks in the Dragoon Mountains.

Supplying the desert with its most prized commodity, windmills pump groundwater on a ranch near Fort Bowie. The remoteness of Cochise County, in Arizona's southeastern corner, made it a haven for outlaws until copper strikes in the late 19th century began to bring law and order, of a sort, to boom towns like Bisbee and Tombstone. The petering out of ore closed most mines by the mid-1970s, but remains from Bisbee's copper deposits —including fine specimens of the minerals azurite and malachite—still herald a heyday for rock hounds. Opposite, retired mining engineer John Schlisser and his wife, Lanie, gather specimens at one of the area's many old mine dumps. Bonanzas from other outings crowd shelves in the Schlissers' Bisbee home, where John examines azurite crystals.

Stately saguaros dwarf bird-watchers scanning the Saguaro National Monument. Unique to the Sonoran Desert, the slow-growing plants can attain heights of 50 feet or more only after two centuries. They play a vital role in the delicate chain of desert ecology, as food or shelter for birds and insects. The prickly pear cactus depends on such animals for cross-pollination during its spring flowering (above, left). Fastest North American bird afoot, the roadrunner outsprints its prey of lizards, snakes, and insects. The cholla cactus (below) has earned fame as one of the desert's spiniest plants.

PAGES 122-123: "White Dove of the Desert," Mission San Xavier del Bac gleams with an intensity matched by the desert sky. Built in 1700, destroyed in an Apache raid, and rebuilt before 1800, it graces the San Xavier Indian Reservation south of Tucson.

Windswept
Ranges of Montana

"The winds may blow/ And the thunder growl/ Or the breezes may safely moan;/ A cowboy's life/ Is a royal life,/ His saddle his kingly throne." These words from a ballad about that most mythic of American figures, the cowboy, may sound corny to real-life ranch hands, but visitors at the Schively Ranch in the Pryor Mountains of south-central Montana often swallow such lyrics like the most delicious of bait. Rather than opt for backpack, canoe, or four-wheel-drive truck, vacationers at the Schively Ranch have chosen to experience the scenic spaces of the West from the classic perch of a horse's back. You name it— freedom, heroism, individualism, high-spirited joy—they're all part of the image of a cowboy sitting tall in the saddle as he rides the high country. Or at least that's what a group of city folks wished to believe on a bright, windy October day as we gathered to take part in a genuine western trail drive.

Photographs by
Scott Rutherford

Outside the corral that first morning, we went through an unaccustomed routine. Norman Mayne, 41, a grocery store owner from Dayton, Ohio, and father of six, was being squeezed into a pair of chaps. Diminutive Ardie Bonanno, 41, also from Dayton and nicknamed the "Winestone Cowboy" because of his wine distributorship back home, was being hoisted into a saddle. "I haven't been on a horse in 25 years," he laughed nervously. "I had to go out and buy all this stuff—boots, chaps, spurs, cowboy hat. And then my wife couldn't handle my new image. On the way to the airport she turned to me and said, 'Will you please take off that stupid hat?' "

Bill Heckerman, 58, a businessman from Jackson Hole, Wyoming, looked the most authentic. He was wearing a blue jean jacket and a belt buckle fashioned from an elk antler. But have you ever seen a cowboy on horseback with a video camera slung from his shoulder? And Bill's 11-year-old grandson, Derek, from the San Francisco Bay area, appeared to have read the wrong brochure. He showed up in a ski jacket, goggles, and a stocking cap.

When introductions between riders and horses had been completed, owner Joe Bassett whistled, waved his hand, and took off on a white horse. The trail drive had begun. Our job was to push 350 head of bawling cattle from their summer pasture in the 5,700-foot-high grasslands of the Pryor Mountains to their lower, warmer, winter quarters 50 miles south, just across the Wyoming line. Joe's instructions were plain: Hold on to the reins; don't run the cattle; and walk if you get sore. "Remember," Joe said, eyeing us from beneath a weathered cowboy hat, "we're not trying to kill anyone. You're here for your vacation."

We immediately pitched into our work. All along a ragged line of Hereford and Angus beef cattle, stragglers were peeling off and heeding their own compasses. We wet-eared cowboys were supposed to chase them back. A dude from Washington, D.C., wearing a felt "Indiana Jones" hat, I sprang to my task. A mother and calf had furtively inched their way up a small bluff and now were breaking into the open. I spurred my charger—a quarter horse, a breed favored by cowpunchers for its sprinting speed and agility. We tore up the hill,

Pinwheel of inky water marks the confluence of Porcupine Creek, lower, and the Bighorn River in Montana's Bighorn Canyon National Recreation Area. Present-day cattle drives through this rugged land offer a taste of the Old West's romance and ruggedness.

rocks clattering, and hit the flat at full gallop. I yelled, waved my hat, and held on. The two dropouts got the message and returned to formation.

This burst of cowboying was exhilarating, a sentiment echoed by Richard Lubejko, an undertaker from Chicago, Illinois, who came trotting up beside me. "This is the real thing," he said happily. "On a regular dude ranch the activities are too programmed. But this is as close to true ranching as I'll ever get. You're paying for this, sure, but there's a purpose to what we're doing."

Concentrating hard on controlling my horse and looking out for straying cattle, I rode for an hour before I began to appreciate just where I was. The herd was moving south across the Crow Indian Reservation, and before me stretched a seemingly endless straw-colored plain. To the sides rose craggy, snow-flecked mountains. The ever present wind carried the scents of leather, cattle, and wide-open spaces. After ten hours and 18 miles on horseback, we halted for the day. When we day-old drovers finally crawled into our sleeping bags inside a large canvas tent, we didn't need to count cows to fall asleep.

Awakened while Venus still blinked in the cold, dark sky, we were soon back in the saddle, combing the surrounding range for any cows that might have wandered from the herd overnight. By midmorning, on what was turning into a glorious Indian summer day, the slow procession had started up again. The hours of the day now stretched out as lazily as did the line of cows, and to keep from dozing in the saddle, we added our noise to that of the herd's, hollering, whistling, singing, or just making conversation.

At one point I found myself alongside Jack Blankenship, one of two hired hands on the drive. Falstaffian in girth and gusto, Jack seemed always to be chasing an errant cow, lassoing the more defiant ones, or cracking a whip over his head. During this brief spell of inactivity, I asked him to define a cowboy. "Well," he pondered, pulling on his bushy beard. "I'll tell you there are lots of fake cowboys who are great at spurring barstools. But people making their living day in and day out on horseback, they are true cowboys." He explained that there are cowmen, too. "A cowboy is basically worried about how wild he can get. A cowman is worried about getting his herd to market and making money."

By the third day of the drive, Bill Heckerman's video footage was going to require editing if he wished to preserve the look of the Old West. Giant wooden poles carrying high-voltage power lines were slicing up the vistas on valley floors. A blacktop road became our trail when the mob of cattle crossed into the Bighorn Canyon National Recreation Area. As if responding to the altered landscape, Joe Bassett, a rancher since 1949, began riding up to his guests and educating us as to how economics can sour a modern stockman's life.

"There's no way you can raise cattle for what you put into them," Joe told me. "Ten years ago I carried 1,200 mother cows. A pickup cost $5,000, a tractor $15,000. Now I have to pay $15,000 for a pickup and $50,000 for a tractor, and I'm carrying half as many cows. I can't afford any more; I have to pay off the bank. And with all the talk about the health effects of beef, we're selling a lot less cows than we used to." Joe went into the guest ranch business as a means of

126

generating more cash flow. His tourist season runs from snowmelt in late April to ice-up in early November, and he offers several roundups and trail drives in the spring and fall. Though our group was exclusively male, Joe assured me that overall, half his guests are female, and that during the summer, he even reserves a week for singles—a sure sign of modern times.

To relieve the languor of the long, hot afternoon, Jack Blankenship proposed a brief detour to see Bighorn Canyon. At a brisk trot, we rode to an overlook where we could run our eyes across the breathtaking gorge cut by the Bighorn River. The sheer walls of the canyon were striped with pale pastels of sedimentary rock. To the south we discerned a distant row of snow-glazed peaks, which Jack reckoned belonged to the Wind River Range, some 150 miles away. We lingered at the vantage point, forgetting for the moment cows, economics, and blacktop roads.

When we caught up with the herd, I joined cowboy Whitey Hopkin, who was riding drag, or in the rear. A laconic, big-boned man, Whitey was pushing the reluctant cows up a dry, twisting gully. The cows' tongues were hanging out; the horses kept losing their footing on the soft slopes as we chased the same cows over and over again; the wind burned our faces; the dust reddened our eyes. Seeing my discomfort, Whitey chuckled, "Yep, this business sure is romantic."

By late afternoon, we reached our destination—the corrals at Crooked Creek, not far from the winter ranch at Lovell, Wyoming. We worked on foot in the stock pens, helping Joe separate his cows from strays that had been swept up in his roundup and were wearing different brands. The sorting did not go like clockwork. The stock trailer got bogged in the mud. Norm the grocer fell ill from dehydration. Jack Blankenship was kicked in the leg by a cow. Not until late at night did we holiday cowboys pull into camp. "We made sure everything didn't run smooth; otherwise you might think you want to live this life," Jack joked soberly, an ice bag on his knee.

A day later, revived by sleep and a plethora of pancakes, we escorted the extra horses back to our starting point in the Pryor Mountains. I was riding Buck, a tireless bay that refused to be headed by his peers. For almost 20 miles I galloped or trotted nearly nonstop before a remuda of a dozen horses, their manes flying in the wind, their yen for home driving them on. At last, I felt that I was on that kingly throne cowboys sing about.

All of us vacationers returned to the Montana ranch a little wiser and a little tougher. What had begun as a joyride had ended up as a heartfelt lesson in the ways of the cattle rancher. We had all learned how to handle a horse, not just sit on one like mannequins on a parade float. And best of all, we honestly felt that we had been of some help. We shaved off our starter beards, put back on our low-cut shoes, and, for a group portrait, posed with our hard-won bowlegged stances. Then we piled into a truck and headed for the Billings airport, Whitey's voice fading after us, "I want you all to eat prime rib every night. . . ."

PAGES 128-129: Men will be boys—cowboys, that is—at the Schively Ranch in Montana's Pryor Mountains. Here guests live out their dreams. A childhood's worth of Saturday matinees inspired him, says white-hatted Norman Mayne, echoing his fellow buckaroos.

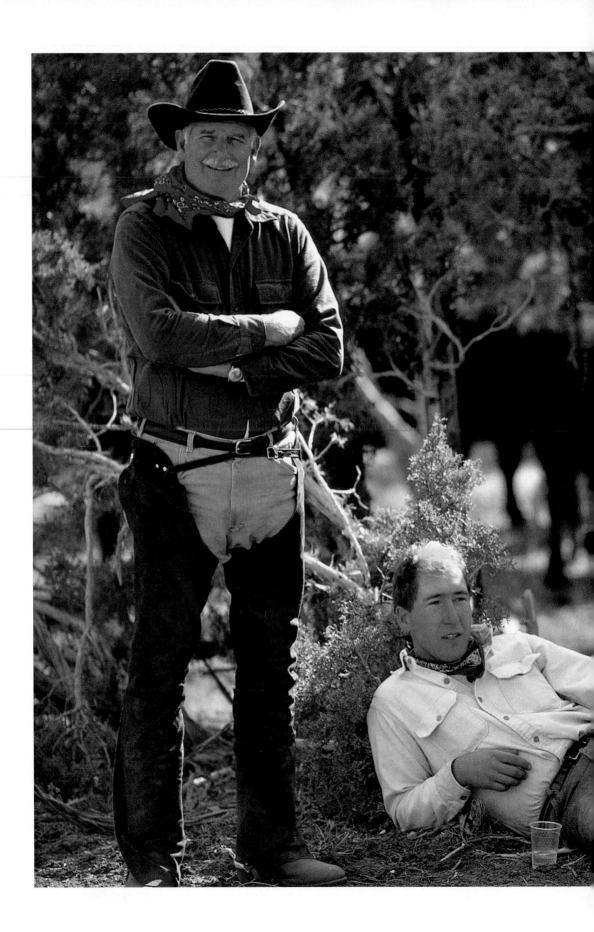

Heading 'em up and moving 'em out, guests of the Schively Ranch coax straggling stock and spare saddle horses along as the working ranch's three-day fall drive begins. The 50-mile trek—from summer pastures in the Pryor Mountains to more temperate winter grounds in Wyoming—winds through the Crow Indian Reservation, Wild Horse Range, and Bighorn Canyon area. In spring, the route is reversed. Above, a wayward Angus tests the herding skills of cowboy Jack Blankenship. At Hough Creek, near trail's end, Jack replaces a lost shoe, while Joe Bassett, owner of the Schively Ranch, steadies the horse.

Home on the range spreads alongside cottonwoods at Deadman Creek (opposite), about 18 miles and a ten-hour ride south of the Schively Ranch. During cattle drives, an advance party bearing trailer-loads of gear and provisions makes camp at each day's rendezvous point. Drovers find hearty campfire-cooked chow ready upon their arrival, prepared from one of the West's few remaining working chuck wagons. First-time cowpokes, unused to a full day on horseback, sometimes look forward most of all to a good night's sleep. Come morning, riders find themselves back in the saddle by dawn's first light. Excitement of the trail behind them, author Tom O'Neill and pint-size hombre Josh Bassett (below) compare headgear at the corrals of Crooked Creek, Wyoming.

PAGES 134-135: Rancher Joe Bassett, at left, and cowboy Whitey Hopkin bring up the drag, or rear, of the trail herd, some 350 head of Hereford and Angus cattle. Whether helping to avert a stampede or rounding up strays, mending fences or feeding calves, guests participate in practically every aspect of life at Schively. "We are not a dude ranch," Joe takes pains to emphasize, but instead, "the real thing."

Untamed
Baja California

Photographs by
Mike Clemmer

What a relief: a flat tire. The once perfect circle of rubber now sat squashed like a piece of broken fruit in the dirt road, stabbed by a cactus spine. Changing the tire would be a hot and dirty business. I had arrived.

To gloat over such a mishap may appear perverse by most lights, but in Baja California, the rugged and remote Mexican peninsula that abuts the state of California, a breakdown seems mandatory if one wants to join the fraternity of authentic Baja travelers. The ruined cars belly-up in gullies, the shrines and white crosses on the roadsides, the mountain of salvaged parts at the occasional village garage all serve notice that across much of Baja, getting there is half the adventure.

The driver of our truck, Norman Roberts, an investment counselor from San Diego, uttered not a curse as he got out the jack and settled into the dust to inspect the damage. As a former bird hunter, onetime racetrack veterinarian, and naturalist, Norm has been frequenting Baja for more than 50 years. He loves it so much that he coauthored and, with his own finances, published a field guide on the peninsula's extravagant vegetation.

"Are we in trouble?" I asked, stamping on a foot pump while Norm, perspiring in the December sun, checked the tire for escaping air. "Naw," he said dismissively. "Hey, Pat, how many flats did we have to fix on that '71 trip, when all those bridges were out?" Pat Flanagan, the other member of our party, a free-spirited biologist who lives in the California desert, dropped the binoculars with which she was tracking a distant hawk and started to count. "Ten, I think, or was it eleven?" She sounded nostalgic.

By the time we had finished with the tire, Norm had recited his Baja casualty list: a truck frame cracked in two places, punctured gas tanks, radiators split from vibration, broken springs, innumerable clogged carburetors, shredded tires. "Not all is lost though when you break down in Baja," Norm concluded, putting his high-domed straw hat back on and starting up the four-wheel-drive camper truck. "Mexican mechanics are great with baling wire."

Traveling through Baja, or lower, California, became immeasurably easier and less stressful with the completion in the early seventies of hard-topped Highway 1, which runs the length of the 800-mile-long peninsula. A low-slung rental sedan, even an ungainly RV, can now reach the sun-splashed resorts at Baja's tip. Before, adventurers in four-wheel-drive vehicles stockpiled with parts and tools had to crawl and bounce over narrow hand-built roads that were often axle deep in sand or strewn with sharp volcanic rocks. The odd thing is, most of the pre-highway travelers loved it. "You were an explorer, not a logistician," sighed one old Baja hand who now leads tours.

The new road is tempting. No longer is a commando's preparation necessary to enjoy the legendary attraction of Baja California: the wild, empty Pacific beaches; lagoons where gray whales calve in winter; island-studded bays in the warm Gulf of California on Baja's eastern edge; villages with adobe houses and

Ultramarine waters of the Gulf of California lap at the desert that defines most of the 800-mile-long peninsula of Baja California. Tall cardon cactus and bushy paloverde climb the sun-baked slopes along this mountain-edged scoop of coastline.

shaded plazas; forests of cactus; dormant volcanoes; sharp-spined mountains that often tumble down to the water's edge. And yet, the highway puts the desert at arm's length, making it seem thornless and empty, not even capable of flattening a tire. Fortunately, nasty, kidney-shaking, unmarked roads still exist. With pleasure I jolted in my seat when Norm pulled off the asphalt south of the settlement of Cataviña and hit the rough ground, disappearing behind a plume of dust as we entered that special Baja realm, the off-road.

We became intimate with the desert really fast. Mesquite branches lashed the sides of the truck. The sprawling arms of thorned shrubs poked through our windows. The farther we went, the more bizarre and enclosing the vegetation became. Multicolumned cardons, tallest of all cactus, grew higher than telephone poles. The elephant tree, *Pachycormus discolor,* sent forth fat, peeling limbs that seemed frozen in a convulsive state. A fright wig of thorns and leaves sprouted the length of the cirio, *Idria columnaris,* a tall, skinny plant that grows almost as high as a cardon—up to 60 feet and more—and whose thin, tapering shape inspired its Spanish name, meaning "candle."

Having spent the previous spring in the barren wastes of the Sahara, I was amazed that an arid climate like Baja's could support such a profusion and complexity of growth. "You pick any spot in this *cardonal,*" Pat said triumphantly as we drove through a forest of cardon, "and count the species in your field of vision. Then go to a northern forest and do the same. It's no contest. This desert has far more species." What's more, absolutely no other place on earth looks like Baja. Of its approximately 110 species of cactus, 85 grow nowhere else, principally because of the peninsula's biological isolation. *Pachycormus,* among other plants, is also considered unique to Baja.

On the unbeaten path we followed, we met some unusual people who inhabit the desert. A wisp of smoke and the sight of a shack made out of cardon ribs and tin sheeting led us to Heliodoro Arce Villavicencio, a short, grizzled man with hardly a tooth in his head. A woodcutter by profession, Heliodoro graciously poured us coffee from a smoke-blackened pot. We admired his homemade cowhide shoes, their soles made from the remains of a flat tire. Seeing our interest, he brought out two new pairs and before long had completed a sale with Pat. The method of pricing was unusual: 1,500 pesos (about three dollars) per shoe. Pat took two. Heliodoro then presented us with a jar of molasses-dark honey he had collected from a hive nearby. We gave him some fresh fruit and, with friendship thus sealed, drove off.

An hour later we stopped again and set off on foot up an arroyo floored with deep white sand. Garage-size boulders perched precariously on the steep hillsides. We soon came to the head of the canyon and there gazed reverently at a pool of tea-colored water shaded from the sun. A semipermanent pool of water might not seem significant elsewhere, but in Baja's central desert, we approached it like pilgrims at a shrine. The rock catchment, historically known as Tinaja de Yubay, held the only water within several days' walk. To reach it we had briefly followed a depression worn into the stone, a path made by footsteps of 18th-century missionaries and by generations of Indians before them.

While Norm and I relaxed and snacked on cheese beneath a fig tree improbably growing from a rock wall, Pat clambered about the vicinity. She soon called excitedly to us from above the pool. We followed her into a low cave where, on our backs, we looked up at walls covered with prehistoric paintings done in reds and blacks. Enigmatic human figures shared the rock face with an array of circles and lines. We fell silent in appreciation.

On the hike back to the truck, none of us said much. By abandoning the solid road we had driven right into the vivid, unforgettable heart of the desert—though sometimes this seemingly overgrown land made me forget exactly where I was. A jungle with thorns, maybe; or perhaps a terrestrial coral reef. But true desert it was: An average of only four inches of precipitation a year reaches Baja's midsection. In some areas not a drop of rain has fallen in successive years. Part of Baja is within the Sonoran Desert, the same one that grips areas of Arizona, southern California, and the Mexican mainland. Of the world's arid realms, the Sonoran Desert contains the greatest variety of flora, and I was witnessing Baja in a particularly lush period that followed several winter storms.

Rain is not the only cause of the greening desert. Camped in a mesquite grove near the remains of the San Fernando Velicata Mission, I stepped out of my tent one morning into a wet blanket of fog. The roof of the tent was soaked. The leaves on the mesquite dripped. *Chi-ca-go, chi-ca-go* quavered the sentinel bird of a large covey of California quail. Several hundred had come down from the hillside above me and were moving nervously through the undergrowth, sipping water from the moist vegetation.

A significant portion of Baja's precipitation in the central desert comes in the form of fog. Dense banks may build up off the Pacific coast where the cold California Current reacts with the warm desert air. The resulting clouds of condensed moisture then drift overland, though, as in southern California, the sun usually burns off the fog by midday. When this morning's gauze cleared, I joined Norm and Pat in searching for flowers. Conditioned to believe that the desert blooms only in spring and summer, I quickly learned otherwise on a December day. By nightfall we had identified a dozen flowering plants, from the *Agave shawii*, or century plant, with its crown of greenish-yellow blooms atop an elongated stalk, to the lavender blossoms of nightshade.

Just as striking as the desert flowers were the desert beaches, which in Baja are never far away, at least as the hawk flies. At its broadest point between the Pacific Ocean and the Gulf of California, Baja is 125 miles wide, and at its narrowest, near the Bahía de La Paz, only 30 miles. But making a dash for the deep blue sea is another matter. Mountains run the length of the peninsula, making a straight east-west road as improbable as a donkey with wings. A hundred-mile journey from coast to coast may use up all the daylight hours.

Prior to my trip with Norm and Pat, I joined another Baja excursion, this time with five vacationers and guides Piet and Karen Van de Mark from San Diego. On the third day of the trip, taken in early November, our two vehicles left the pavement and headed east toward Bahía de San Luis Gonzaga. Following the rutted tracks of previous travelers, we settled into the drive. Soon Piet, the burly, mustached driver and a Baja guide for 20 years, was describing

139

to us the unlikely road he followed from his native Chicago to Baja California.

"Before I came out here, my only exposure to camping was going to Boy Scout meetings in a Lake Shore Drive high rise and listening to the troop leader read stories about the wilderness," Piet said. Then somewhere he heard about Baja. "The public library had only one book about it. It was by Erle Stanley Gardner, the writer who created the character Perry Mason. Gardner wrote about how, in the 1940s through the '60s, he traveled the peninsula exploring and searching for Indian rock art in the mountains. The trips sounded great."

Duly inspired, Piet and some friends drove to California and then down into unpaved Baja. They hunted for food with rifles and sometimes went without; they rationed their water; and they broke down more than once. "If we had known how rough it was, I don't think we would have come," Piet remembered. "I'm sure glad we didn't know."

Shortly before sundown we reached Bahía de San Luis Gonzaga. After the dusty terrain we'd been driving through, the hue of the water stunned us: It was the sensuous royal blue of a fine Persian carpet. A single fishing boat bobbed on the wind-tossed surface, while in the distance an island as gnarled as a walnut jutted up. On the wide, curving beach at the bay's northern end, a fishing camp of sheds and trailers was strung out like sea wrack. Pelicans and frigate birds cruised overhead.

Everyone needs an I-remember-it-when place, some remote, undiscovered beauty spot, experienced in its unspoiled state before developers inevitably come crashing in. Bahía de San Luis Gonzaga qualified for me. I learned later that the Mexican government has its eye on the bay as a potential resort site, but as yet has been unable to find potable well water nearby.

The day after next, our mini-convoy returned to the pavement. For emergencies, Piet carried an extra 30 gallons of gasoline and 20 gallons of water. Though Mexico is one of the world's major oil producers, half of the service stations we passed were boarded up or out of gas—and unleaded gasoline is almost impossible to find. Water was less of a problem, curiously enough: tap water was available at most service stations, schools, and village squares.

Having started our trip in San Diego, we did not see wilderness vistas until we had passed beyond the cities of Tijuana and Ensenada. Then the mountains and the desert took over, interrupted only occasionally by villages and cooperative farms or ranches. At least once a day we passed a Green Angel, the name given the compact green trucks furnished by the Mexican government to patrol the highway and provide assistance to travelers. According to a Green Angel driver I met, the greatest hazard on the Baja blacktop is not cliff plunges, *banditos,* or dust storms, as the uninitiated often fear, but the homely threat of a burro or cow wandering into a vehicle's path.

The first road to invade the Baja desert, traces of which still exist, was built more than 250 years ago by Jesuit missionaries and an army of Indian laborers. Called El Camino Real, the royal road, it linked a network of missions founded in the name of the Spanish crown. In colonizing Lower California, the missionaries succeeded where nearly two centuries of attempts by soldiers and conquistadors, greedy for gold and pearls, had failed. The first mission chapel was dedicated at Loreto, on the Gulf coast, in 1697, to be followed by nearly 30 others during the next 140 years, two-thirds of them founded by Jesuits, the rest by Franciscans and Dominicans who arrived later.

The Indians that the friars believed they were saving presented a formidable challenge. The men went naked, the women bare-breasted; the Indians slept in the open or in caves; they believed in medicine men; and they spent most of their waking hours searching for food, which included lizards, snakes, deer, and cactus fruit. Their language contained no words for hope, love, virtue, or faith. Gradually, however, most of the native population succumbed to the foreigners in robes—the calm, strange-sounding men who, the Indians soon saw, could intimidate their shamans, provide the people with pozole, a sort of stew, and entertain them with rituals full of talking and singing.

Of the more than two dozen mission churches, nearly all lie in ruins. By 1860 all had been abandoned. Diseases brought by the white man had decimated the Indians, and the few missions that remained were gradually closed by the Mexican government. Fortunately, six impressive examples of mission architecture survive, at San Borja, Santa Gertrudis, Mulegé, San Luis Gonzaga, San Javier, and San Ignacio. Many have undergone some restoration and, in their massive and sometimes ornate building style, all preserve a sense of the indomitable faith that upheld the padres and awed their converts.

On a warm, gusty day, Piet led our group off-road from Loreto, the vehicles climbing into the Sierra de la Giganta to the mission of San Javier. On its only street, a broad sandy lane, a few boys were playing baseball. Goat bells chimed atonally from behind a row of low adobe houses. We walked to the end of the road and there gazed up at the symmetrical gray bulk of the church, completed in 1758 and preserved in its original state. Constructed of thick volcanic rock, which must have required a prodigious human effort to quarry and transport, the church stands as a monument to the order and hope that the friars tried to impose on the wilderness.

A dark-haired señora with two children clinging to her skirt unlocked the heavy wooden door and motioned us inside to a cool, dim cavern. "A priest comes once a month from Loreto," the woman whispered in Spanish as our footsteps resounded on the rough stone floor. Another key unlocked a side room, a small museum. In a closet behind glass hung richly designed vestments of the early missionaries. I imagined a mission father standing in these robes before the high gilded altar and facing his hard-won congregation—a group of uncomprehending Indians muttering among themselves, craning their necks to gape at the lofty ceiling.

We left the empty church, and outside on the grounds the señora consented to ring a bell in the tower. She tugged on a rope and a deep brassy boom echoed off the barren hills. A silence even deeper followed us out of town.

The character of Baja begins to shift below Loreto, about two-thirds of the way down the peninsula. Commercial airlines can land here, bringing quick infusions of people. At La Mision Hotel bar I watched a group of festive Americans call for more *cerveza,* or beer. They were wearing clothes strange to the desert: fedoras, backless dresses, clean white pants. A mariachi band blared its version of a José Feliciano song. At the front desk I saw snapshots of sunburnt tourists standing beside enormous fish they had caught. A credit card, I realized, had become handier than a spare fuel tank.

The terrain looked different, too, as we continued south, toward the Tropic of Cancer. Instead of gaunt ravines, the highway passed hillsides choked with leafy plants. Rainfall had become generous. We also became more conscious of the beaches, of how seductively long and deserted they appeared.

Wilderness completely surrendered to playground at the peninsula's tip, a 50-mile stretch of sand, cliffs, and turquoise water, packaged as paradise by a host of resorts. Most of the tourist activity is concentrated around the village of Cabo San Lucas, at the dramatic point where the waters of the Pacific intermingle with the waters of the Gulf of California. Plush, hidden hotels command vistas of endless beaches. Boutiques sell anything from sombreros to jewel-encrusted ceramic skulls. Hotel lobbies advertise sportfishing trips, aerobics classes. Everyone magically speaks English.

Despite a preference for the desert, which demands more involvement than the laid-back resorts, I settled painlessly into my new environment. At dawn at the Hotel Hacienda resort, I would walk from my room into a garden of hibiscus where hummingbirds hovered, then down to the beach and into the warm, buoyant water, pelicans gathering to float alongside me.

In these clear waters where pleasure craft and cruise ships now moor, pirates once lay in wait for Spanish treasure ships returning from the Philippines. As I left Baja, I took with me a wondrous treasure of my own, one shared by my traveling companions Norm and Pat. We drove west out of the oasis of San Ignacio one morning, my friends refusing to divulge our destination. We rattled our way down primitive roads not drawn on any map. The sun pounded a sere landscape that looked like the aftermath of a burn.

On a rough, rock-strewn grade, we came grille to grille with an abandoned pickup left stranded in our path. There was no room to pass, as the roadside bristled with cactus. We ended up attaching a chain to the pickup's frame and yanking the truck off the road.

Sweating freely now, we held on as our truck struggled up the hill. Then we saw it, a glint of primary color, a flash of blue. In the middle of a stark, heat-blasted desert we stared out over a stream, a still ribbon of water flanked by palm trees. Cattle grazed on green meadows. A great blue heron flew from some reeds. "A touch of the wand," Pat exclaimed. Flowing from a pond at San Ignacio that is fed by underground water, the stream runs miraculously for 13 miles before disappearing into salt flats.

Calmly, we stepped out of the truck and climbed down a cliff of loose rocks. Then we gave in. We tore off our clothes and with elated yelps plunged into the cold mossy water. Ah, the desert.

Animals painted by ancient artists skitter over the head of guide Oscár Fischer in El Ratón Cave, midway down the peninsula. Elsewhere in Baja's rugged sierras, life-size murals up to 100 feet long bespeak the sophistication of a mysterious pre-Spanish culture.

Dusting of lacy blooms softens gnarled branches of an elephant tree (opposite, rear), named for its massive trunk. In the foreground grow lancet-leaved agaves and a many-armed cholla cactus. At least 2,500 plant species, and more than a hundred cactus varieties, grow in the Sonoran Desert, which includes parts of Baja. Undaunted by July temperatures exceeding 100°F, Jean Evanich (right) gingerly loosens a ripened fruit of the senita cactus to examine its seeds, afterward spilling the seeds on the ground so they can germinate naturally. Below, other aficionados of desert botany pause to examine a candelilla, or slipper plant.

Off-the-beaten-track means most of Baja, including a rutted road negotiated by a lone vehicle on the peninsula's east side. Since 1973, blacktop Highway 1 has whisked travelers all the way to southernmost Cabo San Lucas, but the adventurous—a goodly proportion of those who journey here—remain steadfast shunpikers. Moreover, notes the author, a breakdown seems mandatory for anyone who would join the fraternity of Baja travelers. If a mishap occurs on the main road, one of the government's brightly colored "Green Angel" service trucks (opposite) often miraculously appears. Despite its hardships, or perhaps because of them, Baja exudes a fascination. As John Steinbeck, who explored it in the 1940s, wrote: "If it were lush and rich, one could understand the pull, but it is fierce and hostile.... But we know we must go back ... and we don't know why."

Fanned by rustling palms, sunbathers bask on the terrace of Hotel Palmilla at Los Cabos, at the tip of the peninsula. Thanks to the completion of Highway 1 and a new airport at nearby San José del Cabo, Baja's remote land's end now boasts a thriving tourist industry centered on a bevy of low-key resorts. Above, Irene Dortch, a guest at Hotel Palmilla, finishes a day of snorkeling on a large coral reef that marks the meeting of the Gulf of California and the Pacific Ocean. Other activities here include superb scuba diving, sportfishing, and boat rides to private beaches known as playas del amor—all of which make the workaday world seem a thought for a distant mañana.

ISLANDS AND COASTS:

WHERE LAND MEETS THE SEA

By Cynthia Russ Ramsay

IRA BLOCK

Virgin Island
Paradise

*Photographs by
Ira Block*

ay after balmy day was a dream come true. Everywhere I looked across the sapphire water I saw a panorama of islands, where palms shade immaculate white beaches, where hibiscus and bougainvillea flowers are as common as dandelions, and under a tropic sky filled with stars, people dine and dance.

At night, as our boat bobbed gently at anchor, the waves whispered softly against the sides. Early in the morning, when the rising sun had separated the deep curve of the shore from the pale green shallows, I slipped into a sea so mellow I felt no chill at all—only a languorous, silky wetness. Back on board, the aroma of coffee and breakfast brought me still dripping to the galley. Then, lolling on deck with the sun warm on my back, I was ready to spend another day cruising the Virgin Islands. Photographer Ira Block, five companions, and I were roaming the Caribbean, dropping anchor at deserted coves or mooring at uncrowded marinas—stopping wherever beauty and adventure beckoned.

My visit to the U.S. Virgins began with a week-long cruise aboard *Freestyle*, a 50-foot trimaran. Her triple hulls provide more stability and more room than traditional sailing vessels. Designed for comfort, she does not perform well to windward, but engines give the sails extra power to head for any destination.

Skipper Bill Hawes, a wiry, imperturbable man who has been sailing for more than half his 24 years, knew every anchorage on the three main islands—St. Thomas, St. John, and St. Croix—and on the 50 or so islets and cays that are also part of the American Virgins. Our meandering course took us briefly into the British Virgins, a cluster of some 30 islands just to the east. Together, these lovely fragments of land comprise the northern end of the Lesser Antilles, an archipelago of drowned volcanic mountains that curve for some 700 miles to the coast of South America and separate the Atlantic from the Caribbean. Only St. Croix lies apart from the chain—across a 40-mile stretch of water to the south. Otherwise, the Virgins form a close succession of green heights, long promontories, and deeply indented coves that create a maze of channels and passages celebrated as among the world's best sailing grounds.

"The prevailing winds—the Easterly Trades—are dependable," Bill told me at the start of our voyage. "Navigation is simple. You don't even need a compass because you can always take your bearing from land. And the next anchorage is as near or as far as you want it to be."

We set out from the storied St. Thomas harbor of Charlotte Amalie, a city of 12,000 that was once a Danish center of commerce and an 18th-century rendezvous for pirates—a place where they refitted their ships and sold their booty. The talent for shrewd trading survives, and the capital of the U.S. Virgins is a flourishing duty-free port that draws more than 1,200 cruise ships a year.

While we were still within the wide harbor set in an amphitheater of hills, *Freestyle*'s cook, blonde, gravely charming Nancy Locke, plied us with a fruity rum concoction and spicy marinated shrimp. On deck, shaded by a blue

Balmy weather and unspoiled sands of St. John's Salomon Beach spell a perfect hideaway. St. John, St. Thomas, and St. Croix—acquired from Denmark in 1917—form a U.S. Territory; northeast of St. John lies the Crown Colony of the British Virgin Islands. PAGES 150-151: St. John's Caneel Bay resort offers luxury living in a jewel-like setting.

awning, I savored my cold, sweet drink and the legendary setting of steep mountains embracing a sea so blue it seemed to blanch the sky. From the distance, bustling Charlotte Amalie remained an appealing West Indian city with shuttered, pastel houses fanning out over the emerald hills. In late September the flamboyant trees still wore a canopy of red flowers that flared like scarlet parasols raised against the sun. Just beyond the narrow, cobbled streets winding uphill from the waterfront, I could see two round stone towers—landmarks known as Bluebeard's Castle and Blackbeard's Castle. Both were, in fact, built as fortifications by the Danish government in the late 17th century.

At the eastern end of the harbor, a grove of masts marked the Yacht Haven Marina, where many of the island's fleet of more than 200 professionally crewed yachts were moored. I learned that a typical boat on a charter with six or eight passengers provides a vacation that costs less than a stay at a first-class resort. There are more opulent vessels, such as the *Bonheur,* which is appointed with television, stereo, whirlpool bath, tables set with silver, crystal, and fine china, and vases filled with a $500 order of fresh flowers for each trip.

"All we have on our table are plastic plates and the food we've cooked ourselves. But I don't think anyone is having a better time," Walter Neuman, Jr., told me when I visited the 33-foot sloop-rigged *Noa Name,* which he and his son were sailing themselves. Occasional weekend sailors who do not own a boat, Neuman and his son, Walter III, had saved for two years for their two-week bareboat charter. "I'd rather handle it all myself," said the elder Neuman, who began his nautical career at 18. "I feel a special harmony with the sea when I'm the one who is gauging the breeze, trimming the sails, and manning the tiller. It's a complete getaway where I can totally relax. There are no phones, no newspapers, no schedules, and no need to dress for dinner."

Near the end of their holiday, the Neumans encountered two soggy days of heavy winds and rain as Hurricane Isabel skirted the Virgins in October. Such tropical storms may strike in late summer and early fall, but for the most part the weather even at this time of year promises smooth sailing. The advantages of lower prices and few boats in the anchorages during this off-season make the risk worth taking, say the Neumans.

I met the Neumans in Leinster Bay, a lunch stop on a route that had taken *Freestyle* along the scalloped north coast of St. John. All morning we had beat to windward on short tacks, motor-sailing past verdant heights that plummet to tranquil coves and crescents of sand. Nature prevailed on the steep slopes, where there were almost no houses; scrub trees had reclaimed hillsides once stripped of their forest cover and planted with sugarcane, cotton, and tobacco, wherever the ground would hold a stalk.

With the creation of Virgin Islands National Park in 1956—from 5,000 acres donated by Laurance S. Rockefeller—nearly two-thirds of St. John was protected from the resort hotels and condominiums that rim the shores of St. Thomas and St. Croix. We saw more pelicans, dive-bombing for fish, than people. Instead of sun-bronzed glamour girls in bikinis, Ira photographed pale donkeys ambling along the beach—descendants of the animals that were the only means of transportation for most of the population until the 1950s.

History, however, has left a few conspicuous marks. Ruins of sugar mills are reminders of the era when the Danes divided the island into about a hundred plantations. Another relic, the old Customs House, stands on Whistling Cay a scant few hundred yards off St. John's shores, at the entrance to the Narrows—a passage that opens into the Sir Francis Drake Channel. From this strategic post the Danes tried to control smuggling from the British islands that flank the 30-mile-long waterway.

Our first stop in the channel was the Bight—a wide, shallow bay of Norman Island. Following Bill's instructions, deckhand Nathan Malkenson swung the anchor overboard and let out about four feet of chain for every foot of water depth. "We need enough scope, or play, so if the wind picks up, we won't start dragging," Bill explained. The sun was setting by the time we lay safely anchored in 40 feet of water near the stony bluffs at the head of the bay. The organ-pipe cactus, which grew from crevices like giant candelabra, cast long, branching shadows across the amber rock face. Across the channel, scattered pinpoints of light proclaimed the presence of people on the rumpled coast of Tortola, largest of the British Virgins. On uninhabited Norman Island, the fast-fading sunset brought the pelicans, terns, and brown-and-white boobies to roost, and the bats swarmed out of trees with a soft rustle of wings.

In the Bight itself, three or four lights winked on, revealing the low silhouettes of boats nearby. In high season—from mid-December through April—there might be as many as 80 yachts moored here. One vessel remains at semipermanent anchor. It is a twin-masted wooden trader painted black and ornamented with white arches and checkerboard panels. After hauling cargo for 70 years, the *William Thornton* has been transformed into a floating bar and restaurant. Nathan ferried us over in *Freestyle*'s motorized dinghy to sample the barman's celebrated rum painkiller—"a tonic . . . not yet available from Druggists and Apothocaries." We returned to *Freestyle* in velvet darkness, and under a sky silvered by the luminous glow of the Milky Way we retold tales of our idyllic day.

We swam and snorkled at almost every stop, finding the exquisite creatures of the coral reef endlessly enchanting. Bill, who was combination skipper, hotel manager, handyman, and tour guide, would lead us through gardens of branched elkhorn and domed brain corals, past filigreed sea fans and feathery gorgonians—the conspicuous structures of the reef.

In the Bight, I donned mask and fins and trailed after Bill. Grunts striped in blue and yellow, groupers with red spots, wrasses with blue heads, snappers with pink lips and fins flitted in and out of view in the marvelously clear water. I was always on the lookout for angelfish and butterfly fish, for their wide, ultra-slim bodies were made even more remarkable by their bold markings and sumptuous colors. I hovered over a dense stand of supple sea whips—a species of gorgonian, or soft coral—and watched the passing parade. Parrotfish, resplendent in iridescent blues, pinks, and greens, glided through purple branches that swayed with the surge of the sea. A dense school of tiny, glassy fry shimmered by. They parted for a moment in response to some mysterious signal and quickly regrouped. Black-banded sergeant majors, the most common fish of these reefs, cruised past, moving with stately calm.

Just then Bill touched my arm and signaled me to follow. For a short while we kept up with a large sea turtle paddling languidly along until it banked, showing its white underside, and left us far behind. A curious thing was the constant, low crackling sound, like cold cereal popping in a bowl of milk. It was made by parrotfish scraping and crunching coral with their beaklike teeth as they grazed on the algae growing on the limestone formations.

On my return to St. Thomas, I enjoyed the spectacle of the reef without getting wet, on a visit to the Coral World Undersea Observatory. With curator Tom Nunn, I descended a circular staircase to the bottom of a tower sunk 15 feet into the sea. "Some corals and sponges were transplanted around the observatory, but the fish are free to come and go as they choose," explained Tom as I entered the twilight darkness of the circular room. Each of the 24 windows, like a magic looking glass, gave me a clear closeup view of a wonderland, and once again the flamboyant fishes enthralled me.

Tom, a marine biologist who moved here from Massachusetts in 1982, commutes to work a hundred yards by dinghy, arriving in T-shirt and shorts. He doesn't own a tie. Casual dress and a blissful climate are part of the laid-back, tropical life-style that has drawn thousands to settle in what the territory's license plates proclaim as the "American Paradise."

Relaxing—"limin" or "coolin out" in the lilting island Creole—is practically a national pastime. "Even the fast-food places are incredibly slow. You either slow down yourself, or you get ulcers," said Tom. The pace does quicken when cruise ships disgorge their throngs intent on shopping sprees. St. Thomas prospered on trade long before the United States purchased the Virgin Islands from Denmark in 1917 for 25 million dollars—ever since 1724, when the Danish crown declared Charlotte Amalie a free port.

On St. John in those days, when rum was the gold of the Caribbean, men made their fortunes on sugarcane cultivated by slaves from Africa. St. John was also the scene of one of the first slave rebellions in the hemisphere. Erupting in November 1733, it took eight months and the intervention of French troops from Martinique to suppress. Emancipation, which came in 1848, hastened the demise of the island's sugar-based economy, already in decline because production from the European sugar beet was driving down prices. In 1955, not more than 700 people remained on St. John. They were subsistence farmers who grazed livestock, caught enough fish to feed themselves, and tended small vegetable gardens. Electricity was available only six hours a day; there were no paved roads; and the district nurse traveled on horseback to deliver babies.

St. John was shaken out of its slumber by the tourist boom beginning in the late 1950s. But with so much of the island protected by the national park—today grown to include some 7,000 acres—there has been no runaway development, and the rustic character of St. John lingers on, though only a 20-minute ferry ride separates the island from the bright lights and hubbub of St. Thomas.

My ferry docked on St. John at the low-key little town of Cruz Bay and left me a few steps from a small park planted with palms, flaming hibiscus, and white false gardenias. Dark-skinned housewives with arms akimbo chatted in the sun-dappled shade. Clusters of taxi drivers gossiped while waiting for fares, exchanging leisurely greetings and laughter with those who sauntered by. A food vendor arranged meat-filled turnovers on a yellow cart. In the early morning, the sidewalks still belonged to the local citizens, but at the cafe flanking the park, a waiter was already wiping tables, awaiting the day's first tourists.

On hilly St. John, rental jeeps are commonly used for sightseeing, and on the scenic but tortuous North Shore Road I drove most of the way in second gear. Rounding steep, sharp curves, I caught glimpses of white beaches and turquoise waters below and wooded islands beyond.

About six miles from Cruz Bay, near the end of the road, I pulled into the Maho Bay Campgrounds. Waiting for me was Resident Manager Bob Berner. A buoyant, energetic man, Bob had been an automobile auctioneer in Florida. "I was making nothing but money, and I wanted memories," he told me as I followed him on the boardwalk that runs through the entire resort and leads down to the beach. At one point the wooden walkway curved right around a tree.

"A deep concern for the environment dominated the design and construction of the complex," Bob told me. "Not a tree or shrub was chopped down. Instead of bulldozing roads for trucks, workers hauled building materials in by hand. The boardwalks were put here to protect the fragile vegetation. Otherwise, the exposed soil washes away in torrential runoffs during a hard rain."

Bob unzipped the doorway flap of one of the unique tent-cottages, and we stepped inside canvas walls supported by wooden beams. The simple furnishings included a camp stove, electric lamps, and an ice chest that served as a refrigerator. Jugs held drinking water, and showers were available in the communal bathhouse a few yards away. The campground offers a relatively low-cost entrée to the island, and despite the modest facilities there is abundant luxury in the setting.

The ultimate in luxury living awaits vacationers at posh Caneel Bay—a resort of subdued elegance set in 170 manicured acres of flowering shrubs and nestled beside seven secluded beaches. When I arrived, guests were feasting on a luncheon buffet that included cold passion-fruit bisque, artichokes vinaigrette, and papaya stuffed with conch or lobster salad.

From the beachside terrace dining room I watched two people on sailboards skim across the bay with enviable ease. I had tried to master the sport, but lifting the heavy sail out of the water and holding the mast upright for a few seconds seemed all I could manage before toppling over backward. The blond, fresh-faced beach supervisor assured me I could learn. "After all, I taught a 70-year-old lady to windsurf," he said, attempting to bolster my determination. A proficient board sailor leans far back to brace his body against the weight of a wind-filled sail. I never mastered that bold style, but for the few minutes I controlled the boom and was able to tilt the mast to catch the breeze, it was magic—with all the thrill of skiing and the challenge of sailing.

Leaving the paradise of Caneel Bay, I headed for St. Croix—aboard a "Goose," one of the seaplanes shuttling between the islands. We took off from Cruz Bay and in 20 minutes splashed down in the harbor of Christiansted, largest town on this island of 50,000. As the plane plowed through the light swells to the landing ramp, I could see why the town had the reputation for having one of the most picturesque waterfronts in the West Indies. With its enclave of 18th-century yellow brick buildings, including a massive fort with ancient cannon still pointing out to sea, the city retains the look of its colonial past. Even close up, on its arcaded sidewalks, Christiansted preserves a quaint Old World ambience in contrast to the big city brashness of Charlotte Amalie.

"Only 124 cruise ships came to St. Croix in 1985," said vivacious Shelly Lauterbach, co-owner of a new craft and jewelry shop. "Here you pay up to $10,000 for the privilege of buying a lease; on St. Thomas it costs $50,000. But I don't want to make a lot of money—just pay my bills. If my business fails and I lose every cent I've invested, it will have been a great vacation. After all, I'm learning to sail; I'm getting better as a diver; and I have more time with my daughter."

The island abounds with beaches, and if they aren't enough, Buck Island, with its powdery sands and famed reef, is only a pleasant boat ride away. Our sloop dropped anchor at the beginning of a marked underwater trail, and from the boat I could read a sign: "Don't Stand on the Coral." The park service attempts to protect this fragile ecosystem, declared a national monument in 1961.

A visitor to St. Croix can always retreat from the noonday sun with excursions into history. The ruins of sugar mills are everywhere. There are 114 of them; each plantation built its own, for it was important to squeeze the cane as soon as it was cut. There is the Whim Greathouse, a neoclassic white manor house restored to its 18th-century elegance and filled with fine furnishings that tell of prosperity sustained by the labor of slaves. On the west end of the island, the architecture of the town of Frederiksted tells of labor riots in 1878. Many buildings, which strike the eye with their late Victorian gingerbread style, were constructed after workers burned much of the town to the ground.

At Sprat Hall, completed by 1670 and now a resort, I sampled a bit of plantation living—sleeping in a great mahogany four-poster, sipping rum punch on a broad veranda surrounded by flowers, and setting out by horse for a ride through the cool heights of the nearby rain forest.

The trail I followed led past graceful rain trees with great arching canopies. I saw broad-buttressed kapoks hung with black pods filled with fluff and a random profusion of fruit trees bearing mangoes, genips, sugar apples, and soursops. There were pungent turpentines, locally called tourist trees because of their red, peeling bark. In places, vines cascaded from branches like rain.

I came to a meadow, high on a knoll overlooking the Caribbean. In the quiet enchantment of the sunset, I watched the rust-red disk slipping out of the sky. I was hoping to catch sight of the fleeting, mysterious "green flash" that occurs at sea just the instant before the sun completely disappears. I missed it, perhaps because my mind was beguiled by so many bright memories—of golden days and mellow evenings among these tranquil isles.

Overlooking Christiansted harbor on St. Croix, cannons of Fort Christiansvaern—emplaced to drive off pirates—never resounded in battle. Today the 18th-century fort and other buildings make up a National Historic Site honoring the island's Danish legacy.

Getting down to island basics, vacationers at Caneel Bay bask away their daylight hours. In addition to sailing, diving, and other water sports, island guests may opt for tennis or a hike in emerald-cloaked hills that rise from sparkling white beaches. St. John's history also beckons visitors. Located in the national park that preserves most of the island, the ruins of Annaberg sugar mill hark back to the early 1700s, when a hundred Danish plantations flourished here. Opposite, a snorkeler splashes ashore in the crystal waters of lush Trunk Bay, where markers along an underwater trail identify corals and fish.

161

*Slicing through shallows off St. Thomas, the
50-foot trimaran Freestyle carries up to eight
passengers in addition to a crew of three. Boat
charters—ranging from bareboats to fully crewed
packages—enable vacationers to sample the Virgins
at their own pace, dropping anchor wherever they
choose. Slower but more stable and roomier than
a single-hull boat of equal length, Freestyle's triple-
hull design boasts 1,500 square feet of deck, four
guest cabins with queen-size berths, a main salon
and full galley, as well as a wheelhouse, cockpit,
and crew's quarters. Above, ship's cook Nancy
Locke and deckhand Nathan Malkenson wrestle
with Freestyle's rainbow-hued jib, while a passenger
(right) seeks more restful pursuits atop a trampoline
between two of the boat's hulls.*

Afloat in shimmering waters, a snorkeler explores boulder-strewn shallows of The Baths, edging British Virgin Gorda. Off The Baths' dazzling beaches, corals grow on the sandy bottom. Throughout the islands, reefs support a wealth of fish. Opposite, left, swim blackbar soldierfish; opposite, right, grunts (top) and squirrelfish school near a red hind.

PAGES 166-167: Jumbled, house-size granite boulders—their origin a mystery amid these isles born of volcanic activity—create quiet pools that earn fame for The Baths.

Nantucket and Martha's Vineyard

Photographs by
Stephen R. Brown

30-mile trip aboard a ferry took me back to the 19th century. I went from the Massachusetts mainland to Nantucket, an island that was once one of the whaling capitals of the world. As I walked ashore in Nantucket town, home port for more than a hundred sailing ships that roamed the globe hunting the sperm whale, I was immediately drawn into the past by graceful old buildings on cobblestone streets and narrow lanes. There were white-pillared mansions and cedar-shingled dwellings weathered silvery gray—all built before 1850 and little changed from the days when whale oil for lamps and spermaceti candles brought boom times to what Daniel Webster called "a city in the ocean."

"Strict building codes try to preserve the look of the past," said Victoria Hawkins, amiable curator of collections at the Nantucket Historical Association. "If you build a house tomorrow, we want it to suit Nantucket's historical character." As we strolled along the tree-lined streets on a crisp September day, bright with autumn leaves, only cars intruded on the otherworldly atmosphere.

I learned that Nantucket's whaling industry had collapsed by 1870, plunging the town into a numbing depression so complete that nearly everything, including construction, came to a halt. Thus, a corner of pre-Victorian America was preserved, providing a rare look at how an early seafaring community once lived. Certainly, the island attracts vacationers with its broad sand beaches and its fine surf fishing and sailing waters; but to the tang of salt air Nantucket adds a special allure—its living history.

On my ramble through town, quiet and uncrowded in the off-season that follows Labor Day, I stepped inside the Nathaniel Macy House, built in 1723. Owned now by the historical association, it is open to the public. The kitchen is long and spacious, with a walk-in fireplace where meals were cooked, and gleaming pewter plates and iron cooking utensils. It conjured visions of women in aprons who kept households and businesses alive while husbands and sons were at sea for two to five years at a time.

Tools of that hard seafaring trade, as well as art and artifacts from Nantucket's golden age, are on display at the Whaling Museum. In one corner, a weathered whaleboat, the jaw of a sperm whale—nearly 18 feet long—and a collection of harpoons called to mind the danger and drama of chases such as those chronicled by Herman Melville in his novel *Moby Dick*. The wounded whale would, in its pain, streak away, towing the boat, "so it flew through the boiling water like a shark," in what came to be known as a Nantucket sleigh ride.

Once a seaman himself, Melville heard the story of an enraged sperm whale that in 1820 charged and sank the *Essex* of Nantucket—a tragedy he immortalized in *Moby Dick*. It wasn't until years later that the author visited Nantucket. Like Melville, I spent the night at the Jared Coffin House, an 1845 brick mansion converted into an inn, where dark antique furniture, oriental rugs, and polished old brass gleamed in rooms warmed by crackling fires.

Next morning I wandered in and out of the more than 15 craft and antique

Masts fade into the mist on a foggy Nantucket morning. As summer people depart, New England's historic Nantucket and nearby Martha's Vineyard settle into a leisurely pace, charming off-season visitors with quiet beaches, quaint towns, and enduring island ways.

shops with offerings of Chinese porcelains, nautical instruments and heirlooms, hooked rugs, and old silver. At almost every stop, I saw examples of scrimshaw—incised whalebone or ivory with the lines colored in. Originally the handiwork of whalers passing time during the long voyages, it now pays the rent for talented craftsmen such as David Lazarus. "Few of the old sailors were artists, so they would trace magazine illustrations, pricking the outlines with a sail needle," said Dave, a young, athletic Englishman who gave up a career as a book illustrator after he saw some scrimshaw while on vacation.

Scrimshaw plaques decorate the lids of Nantucket lightship baskets, which are woven of rattan around a wood base. Once made by crewmen on lightships anchored near treacherous offshore shoals, the baskets are unique to the island. In recent years they have become status-symbol handbags costing as much as $1,500—chic purses from a place that has become an elite summer retreat. Nantucket's popularity as a summer resort has sent real estate sky-high in the past 15 years: Sea captains' homes have sold for more than a million dollars, and 20 acres along the harbor recently went for two million. Some mansions have been converted into inns, where the less affluent can slip away from the 20th century in an elegant Nantucket home.

More Spartan accommodations suited Albert Noreen, who was staying in one of the dormitories set up in a former Coast Guard lifesaving station on the south shore, where tricky coastal waters have claimed numerous ships. An American Youth Hostel, the long, gabled structure houses Elder Hostel programs in early spring and late fall. Albert, age 64 and a retired lieutenant colonel, was part of a group enjoying good fellowship and specially catered food at modest prices. "These Elder Hostels are like kisses. They're all nice, but some are better than others," said Albert. Waving his hand toward the lonely ribbon of beach right outside the door, he added, "This hostel is one of the finest."

I had met Albert on the bike path between Nantucket and the village of Siasconset (always referred to as 'Sconset) on the eastern shore. The seven-mile route took us past stands of scrub oak and pitch pine. Beyond lay the rolling, moorlike meadows where farmers had once grazed their sheep in common herds. The first chills of autumn had tinted the thickets of lowbush blueberry and huckleberry in soft, deep reds that brought a ruddy blush to the landscape.

We did not stop pedaling until we reached 'Sconset, where old fishermen's shanties have been transformed into rose-covered cottages, and the Sankaty Head Lighthouse towers above golf links by the sea. On the scenic bluffs overlooking the Atlantic, we followed a footpath half overgrown with flowers. We gazed at tawny dunes, swaying beach grass, a dark sea scalloped with whitecaps, and a horizon so far it seemed as if we were looking at the world's rim.

From both sides of the Atlantic, gourmets flock to 'Sconset's Chanticleer Inn, a restaurant renowned for its French cuisine. In a garden setting, chef Jean-Charles Berruet creates sublime meals complemented by wines from a cellar ranked among the world's best. The mousse of duck livers in sherry vinegar sauce was so delicious that I asked the chef if he would part with his secrets. "I don't mind giving away my recipes," he replied with a Gallic shrug of his shoulders. "If Picasso gave me paints and canvas, would that make me an artist?"

Most people who live on Nantucket or spend summers there never set foot on Martha's Vineyard, an island about twice as large and only seven miles from "America." Natives and newcomers on the two islands keep up a good-natured rivalry perpetuated in print. *New York Times* columnist Russell Baker says Nantucket-lovers "smile a bit condescendingly" about the fact that you can see the Vineyard from the mainland and get there by ferry in 40 minutes. "Nantucket's people pride themselves on being on a real island. . . . a tiny mound of sand in the angry Atlantic. . . . When you finally arrive you feel far away."

The late Henry Beetle Hough, the Pulitzer Prize-winning writer and editor of the *Vineyard Gazette*, one of the great weeklies of the country, wrote, "Those who have an affection for Martha's Vineyard also like the sea, but tend to believe that a vista is best that has something green and solid in it." For Hough, the Vineyard's diversity with "enclaves among its hills, streams, valleys" sets it far above the "contained homogeneity" of Nantucket.

A ten-minute flight from Nantucket took me to the Vineyard's gentle, rural countryside in a seashore setting. I was driving the road that parallels the south shore. Dense woods of pine and scrub oak gave way to open fields as I neared West Tisbury, one of six townships on the island. A placid millpond with a flotilla of swans and ducks enhanced the pastoral beauty of the scene. Just beyond was West Tisbury's steepled, clapboard church, town hall, and general store—the rustic New England village of everyone's imagination.

From West Tisbury, the South Road traversed the green hills of Chilmark, crisscrossed by low walls of stone cleared from the thin soil. I stopped at Clarissa Allen's sheep farm, set on land that had been in her family for 200 years. Clarissa greeted me in her showroom, which is hung with shawls, blankets, and sweaters in soft, earthy hues. Pointing to the looms and hand-knitting machines in a corner of her shop, she said, "It's satisfying to follow through on the whole process, from raising sheep to manufacturing a finished product."

From her farm, broad vistas brought me my first view of Vineyard beaches and the sea. Many beaches on the island are private, reserved for residents who zealously guard the serenity of their stretch of sand. By mid-September, however, no one was patrolling the parking areas for town stickers. The problem was finding the right turnoff from the main road. Maps do not show the access routes, and it takes inside information to recognize a telephone pole or a boulder with a small red ribbon as a marker.

On the western tip of the island, I came to the lighthouse and the dramatically eroded 130-foot clay cliffs of Gay Head, celebrated for their vivid colors and fossil treasures of whale, camel, and elephant bones millions of years old. Farther on, a narrow, quarter-mile footpath gives the public access to a scenic beach, but I remained up on the lookout, above sunlit shallows dappled by clusters of seaweed. In the distance, goldenrod spangled a field reaching almost to the edge of the still, dark waters of Squibnocket Pond.

A special feature of the island's geography, the many ponds are arms of the sea, walled off by barrier beaches built by currents and tides. "The walls are cut two or three times a year to let in seawater for scallops and clams," John Becker told me as we chugged out of a long, narrow cove into the broad heart of Great Tisbury Pond in a flat-bottomed johnboat. An architect, John had summered on the island since childhood; three years ago, at age 36, he decided to make the Vineyard his home, finding the quiet, the harmony with nature, and the isolation—with a certain proximity to Boston and New York—especially appealing.

A speed limit of ten miles an hour gave us time to watch for ospreys, swans, snowy egrets, and black-crowned night herons, which come to fish in the fertile waters and its fringe of marsh. By the time we pulled up to the dunes and walked onto the white sands of South Beach we had made several sightings.

The large ponds and bays also draw commercial fishermen, who drag the bottoms for scallops during the season, which begins in November. "It's scalloping in winter and lobstering at sea in the summer," said Eric Cottle, an old-timer who used to go after swordfish with hand-thrown harpoons. Eric lives in Menemsha, a small, weathered fishing village with a ramshackle charm. Like a spotlight, the slanting rays of the setting sun cast a single golden stripe across the darkness of Vineyard Sound. The fleet was in, and on the dock lay a piled assortment of nets, buoys, and lobster pots made of oak laths.

The docks of Edgartown and Vineyard Haven were different from those of Menemsha. Sleek pleasure yachts outnumbered wooden fishing vessels, and dusk was more a time for cocktails than for unloading the day's catch. Edgartown, an old whaling port with stately white houses, is considered the most fashionable resort community on the island. Summer homes rent for as much as $30,000 for the three-month season, and boutiques find customers for silk-screened T-shirts, exotic plants, and temple carvings from China.

Actually, all of the Vineyard has become an "in" place, and the island is as famous for its celebrities as for its pristine beauty. Walter Cronkite anchors his yacht at Edgartown; Washington columnist Art Buchwald plays tennis at Vineyard Haven. The editor of *Time,* the owner of the *Washington Post* and *Newsweek,* opera singers, movie stars, and notables from the political and literary world find refuge here. For the most part, Yankee decorum preserves their privacy, and the wonderfully varied landscape offers something for everybody—even campgrounds for those on a limited budget.

On my last morning, I rented a bicycle in Edgartown and set out along a narrow strip of land with Sengekontacket Pond on my left and the beach and choppy Nantucket Sound to the right. Although mopeds and other bicyclists shared the pathway, and cars sped alongside, the voice of the wind, the sound of the water, the immensity of the sky still held sway on the island. Despite its trendy sushi bars, health clubs, and gourmet carry-outs, the Vineyard—like Nantucket—still belongs to the sea and shore.

Like a stroll down memory lane, the streets of Edgartown reflect the easy elegance of Martha's Vineyard. Once a sea captain's home, the Charlotte Inn houses antique-filled rooms, an art gallery, and French restaurant. In front sits the owner's 1940 Ford woody.

PAGES 174-175: A bicyclist pauses to make a friend along the Vineyard's South Road. Bike paths crisscross the island, a scenic medley of beaches, forests, meadows, and marshes.

Salt-tanged sea breezes set boats swinging in Menemsha harbor, a fishing village on Martha's Vineyard. The U.S. flag flutters over a white clapboard Coast Guard station, which features an enclosed widow's walk. In the 1800s, during the heyday of the whaling industry, island wives frequented such house-top lookouts to scan the horizon for their husbands' returning ships. Whalers often spent years at sea, sailing the world's oceans in search of the great sperm whale. Pursuing smaller prey, a grandfather and grandson (opposite) seine for baitfish on Chappaquiddick, a small island just east of the Vineyard.

177

*Reminiscent of seafaring days, a model whaleboat
fascinates visitors at the Nantucket Whaling
Museum. Whaling brought prosperity to the tiny
island. Today the legacy lives on as cobblestone
streets and hundreds of historic buildings sustain
the romance of the 19th century. Built in 1847 as
a factory to produce candles from whale oil, the
museum is one of nine original structures preserved
by the Nantucket Historical Association.*

*Tied into the Renegade's fighting seat, Donnie
Gemmell (above) matches strength and endurance
with a 350-pound bluefin tuna. Wayne Dent, at
left, and captain James Robert assist with the catch
during the 1985 Nantucket Billfish Tournament,
a week-long contest held in the summer. For landing
such big game fish as tuna, marlin, sailfish,
swordfish, and mako shark, sportsmen consider the
Fin-Nor (right) the "Rolls Royce" of deep-sea reels.*

PAGES 180-181: *Under full sail, boats round a buoy
in the Opera House Cup. Open only to wooden
boats, Nantucket's biggest race is held each summer
for a silver trophy and the sheer fun of competing.*

Oregon's Majestic Coast

Photographs by
Scott Rutherford

Horizontal rain. It was blowing so hard the rain was coming down sideways. Wind whipped the procession of breakers into a single band of froth that burst upon the rocky headland in white explosions. Sand was being swept along the beach—the wild flow giving form and substance to the wind. Atop the bluff, pines and spruces, bowed and pruned by seasons of storms, shuddered in the onslaught, while the gulls landing on the balcony rail outside my room stood still as the wind raked and parted their feathers.

It was winter on the Oregon coast—a time when boisterous weather roils the wide, dark Pacific, assails the wooded headlands jutting out into the ocean, and rattles the windows in hamlets and small towns that mark this scenic sliver of America. The untamed nature of this stormy season holds its own fascination, attracting many people who are invigorated by its wildness.

During a journey of several days along the northern half of the coast, from Newport to Cannon Beach, my encounters with the weather were not all stormy. As I followed U.S. 101, the coast highway, past settlements and stretches of undeveloped shoreline, sometimes the blanket of clouds parted to reveal patches of wan blue sky, and the sun, a glare behind the clouds, cast a steely sheen on the water.

One day was utterly clear, with a sparkling sea, and air tonic with fresh, clean breezes. That day, I was watching the Spouting Horns in Depoe Bay, where the crashing waves heaved water through crevices in the rock. The sun's rays brought rainbows to the jets of ocean spray, and as the wisps of vapor fell back to sea, the ribbons of color shrank and disappeared—the geysers and rainbows rising and falling in creations as fragile and ephemeral as a dream.

Sometimes, the local residents told me, you'll get all kinds of weather in one day. "Like the restless ocean, the weather is changing all the time," said novelist Jean Auel, author of such best-sellers as *The Clan of the Cave Bear*. A woman who can live where she chooses, Jean draws energy from the spectacles of nature that are commonplace on the Oregon coast. "Whether it's summer, when it's foggy and mysterious, September, when it's warm and sunny, or winter, when the wind is snapping the branches off the trees, you are always aware of nature out here," she told me. "Whatever the season, it's always so lush and green and fresh. Walking on the beaches or in the deep woods gives me the solitude I need for my writing. I can pull into my own world and let my stories come."

In Cannon Beach, a resort community of 1,200, I sought out Jim and Deborah Hannen, who were in their studio fashioning designs of stained glass. Jim talked as he rolled a glass cutter around paper templates. Originally from Portland, Jim came to the coast for the scenery. "We live beside the ocean with all its awesome power, yet in 15 minutes we can be in a peaceful forest beside a waterfall splashing into a clear stream," said Jim.

Working on the coast has also been good for the Hannens' business. "At home, people are busy with their 9-to-5 jobs. When they're here, they are

Eroded mass of basalt formed by ancient lava flows, Haystack Rock rises 235 feet above water's edge near Cannon Beach, Oregon. Oregon's coast offers year-round spectacles; in winter, dramatic storms, whale watching, and beachcombing enthrall visitors and residents.

more relaxed and have time to look. Some people stop at every shop in town."

Glassblowers, weavers, potters, goldsmiths, sculptors, woodworkers, and painters have settled along this stretch of coast, finding the area both a haven and a forum for displaying and selling their works. Galleries abound—even the tiny village of Nehelem has three. Many feature art from all over the Pacific Northwest, as well as from local studios. Browsing in the galleries—a dozen in Cannon Beach, and many more all along my route—I could not help but feel the vitality of the people living on these wild shores.

Stormy weather did not stop me from setting out on the Siletz River to cast for steelhead—a hard-fighting, good-eating, oceangoing trout that spawns in the streams of the Pacific Northwest. "Weather looks good to me," said fishing guide David Morgans. I looked at the leaden sky with black clouds already bearing down on Cascade Head in the distance. For Dave and other hardy anglers, the first storms of winter mean the beginning of the winter run of steelhead.

"These fish seem to sense the coming of rain, and that's usually when they start moving. They wait for a certain water depth to go upstream," said Dave, as we drove to our put-in point 25 miles up the river. For three hours we fished the Siletz from Dave's drift boat. In the shallow riffles we trolled with rods rigged with diving plugs, and in the smooth deep holes we cast weighted hooks baited with salmon roe.

Nothing. Not a jiggle or a fleeting tap. It's never easy fishing for steelhead, I learned. On the other hand, bottom fishing in the ocean for rockfish, lingcod, halibut, and sea bass greatly improves the odds of landing something. As a matter of fact, it's pretty much a sure thing. "At times, bottom fish get into a biting frenzy. The fastest catch we ever had on one of my boats was 200 in 20 minutes," said Richard Allyn, partner in an ocean sportfishing operation in Depoe Bay. "The slowest was 30 fish in 5 hours."

These days, nearly all commercial boats use a chromoscope to locate the schools. The fish show up on the screen as blobs and dots of different colors. "Sometimes the bottom fish stack up like pancakes in columns 75 feet high. Dropping a line down with three separate hooks, or jigs, really brings results," said Rich. "Although bottom fishing in winter is getting more popular, salmon are still the biggest draw. More than 50 percent of our income is from the salmon season in summer."

Rich and I were standing on the bridge spanning the narrow, rockbound channel leading into Depoe Bay's snug six-acre harbor, known as the Hole-in-the-Wall. On one side was the wild, gray-green ocean with 22-foot swells and with combers bursting into great curtains of spray. From the other side we could look down on the tiny boat basin with a lineup of vessels "rubbing the dock"—unwilling to venture out into the rough water.

"Some of our heaviest seas occur during the nicest weather," said Captain Stan, a ruddy, jovial man and Rich's father and astute business partner. We had joined him aboard the *Tradewinds Kingfisher,* hoping anxiously for a change in ocean conditions. I had planned to go out on one of the increasingly popular whale-watching cruises to see the awesome 40-ton sea mammals on their annual migration south. Gray whales pass the Oregon coast during December and January on their way from arctic waters to their breeding grounds in the lagoons of Baja California. "When they're heading south, they're one to three miles offshore, going lickety-split," said Rich. "Sometimes we have to go at six knots to keep up with them."

"We locate them by their spouts—the plume of moist, warm air they exhale when they come up to breathe," said Captain Stan. "We do our best to stay a legal distance away—100 yards—but whales sometimes surface right alongside, and we can look at their huge tails pumping up and down with tremendous thrusts. Imagine what it's like when these whales catapult themselves out of the water like a trout after a fly and flop back with a tidal-wave *thwack*. You don't see elephants jumping off the ground, yet these whales are ten times as large. Every time we see them we are impressed all over again."

By two o'clock it was definitely no-go for the cruise, and I retreated to the subdued luxury of Salishan, a resort with a scenic 18-hole golf course, indoor swimming pool and tennis courts, and a fireplace in every room. I spent the following day moseying down the coast to Newport, 22 miles south. My first detour took me along the scenic Otter Crest Loop, which winds up to Cape Foulweather overlook. Every turn brought lovely vistas of crashing waves, coves with broad beaches, and a series of offshore crags, where the churning sea spattered the wet, black rocks with surf. At the summit, almost 500 feet above the sea, a bronze plaque tells visitors that Capt. James Cook named the headland after making his landfall on a stormy March 7, 1778. It also notes that winds of a hundred miles an hour can occur here in winter.

Between Cape Foulweather and Newport, on the two-mile stretch of sand called Agate Beach, the roar of the surf drowned the hollow wail of the wind. People were walking dogs. Children ran back and forth in front of their parents. Driftwood littered the beach, transformed by nature into silvery gray abstract sculptures. I found a feather far too big to belong to the sanderlings playing tag with the breakers and probing the backwash for tiny larvae they eat. I did not find the agates for which many Oregon beaches are famous. That takes a practiced eye, for many of the pebbles reveal their lovely colors and translucence only when they are abraded and polished in mechanical tumblers.

In another season I would have sought out a rocky beach for its tide pools—a place such as Boiler Bay to the north. In winter, however, lowest low tides occur when it is too dark to see the teeming life exposed by the ebbing waters. When the waves do recede from the slippery, seaweed-covered rocks, they leave behind quiet, mirrorlike pools where a multitude of fascinating creatures come into view: sponges in electric colors of orange, yellow, and pink; sea cucumbers with underbodies striped by hundreds of tube feet; green sea anemones with stinging tentacles that look like petals of a flower; and orange or purple sea stars that feed by extruding their stomachs onto their prey.

Beachcombing is a big activity on the Oregon coast, and few know more about it than Dave Eisen, a youthful lumber mill worker from Netarts. Dave advises beachcombers to wait for a storm with winds from the west or southwest. "Then you need patience and a keen eye as you walk the tide line. And you can't let rain or 55-mile-an-hour winds stop you," he told me when I visited him on my way back north.

Over the years, Dave has turned up more than 3,000 glass floats used by Asian fishermen to buoy their nets. His finds, which decorate his living room and lawn and fill up his garage, also include cans of U.S. Army emergency drinking water from World War II, a life preserver from Singapore, a Vietnamese lifeboat, and a love letter a Japanese fisherman stuffed into a small jar.

Nothing is for sale. "They mean too much to me," said Dave, showing me some of his more unusual treasures—three clay urns sealed shut. He won't open them. He won't let the University of Washington X-ray or carbon-date them. "Although some people believe they are Okinawan burial urns, I don't want to ruin the mystery."

I came upon other mysteries, as well as legends of treasure, on Neahkahnie Mountain. It rises 1,661 feet—an elevation that makes it the highest peak on the northern half of the coast but does not convey the impact of its sheer vertical ascent from the sea. "Call it the mountain of a thousand holes," said Wayne Jensen, curator of the Tillamook County Pioneer Museum. "Treasure hunters have been digging here since the 1870s. In the last century, the Nehalem Indians told a garbled tale of white men coming ashore and burying a chest," said Wayne, striding through the brush on the lower slopes of the mountain. "There are also rocks with lines carved on them. We've found more than 50 of them. Somebody had a purpose in doing these."

Wayne stopped in front of a low mound of stones. "On top of this pile we found a large stone with a groove in it almost exactly 36 inches long—a measuring rod, if you're using English distances. On another rock mound to the south we found a rock carved with the number 1632. It was almost exactly 1,632 yards away from here," said Wayne in the mild voice of a cautious and methodical man. "Everything we've found seems to be in the pattern of the English triangulation surveys of the 16th century.

"My feeling is that Sir Francis Drake landed here. I believe his map marking Portus Nova Albionis is of Short Sand Cove, on the north side of Neahkahnie Mountain. The white cliffs his journals refer to are the vertical face of Neahkahnie reflecting the afternoon sun. It certainly merits further investigation, for no one has unequivocally identified Drake's harbor."

Or, I thought, the tons of plunder Drake reportedly removed from his ship and stored ashore. The possibilities were intriguing, and I wondered about them as we followed the zigzag trail to the summit. It could be that Neahkahnie will continue to haunt us with its mysteries, just as the wild Oregon coast continues to allure visitors with its majesty.

Hikers tramp an old landslide draping a rocky trail in Ecola State Park, on Tillamook Head. High, jutting headlands prove ideal for sighting whales migrating south from the Bering Sea in December-January and north from Baja California in March through May.

PAGES 188-189: Threading a dangerous channel, Coast Guard boats motor out of tiny Depoe Bay. Pacific storms lashing Oregon's rocky coast keep rescue vessels busy.

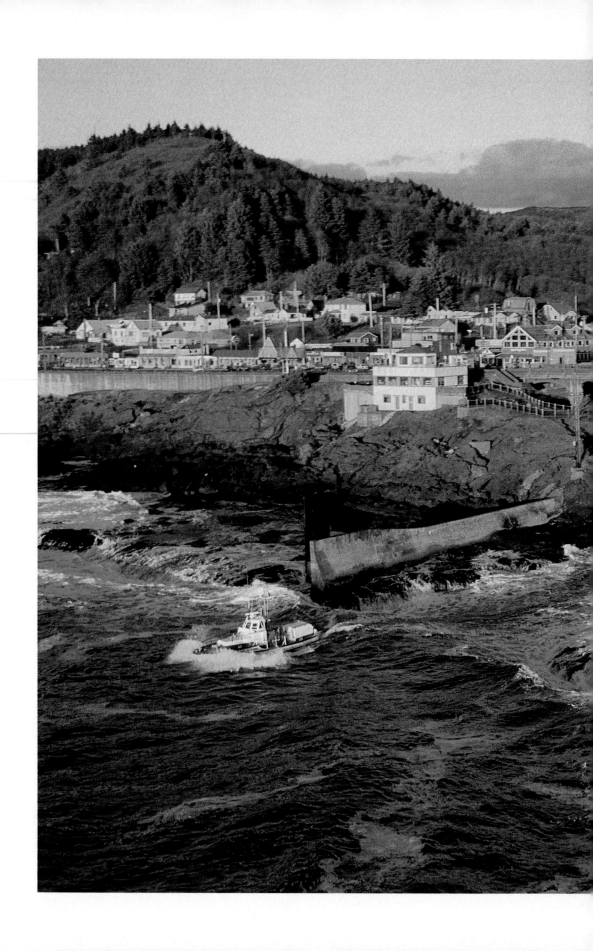

Fresh seafood remains a tantalizing Oregon specialty, whether in working harbor towns or at plush vacation resorts. Robert Pounding, executive chef of the fashionable Salishan Lodge in Gleneden Beach, holds a bounty harvested from Oregon waters: Pacific red rockfish, Dungeness crab, oysters, salmon filets, and crayfish. Yaquina Lighthouse stands on the distant headland. At the counter of a roadside market along Route 101 near Seaside, Beverly Furnish (left) sells Dungeness crabs, known for meat so sweet that butter is unnecessary. The menu at the Lazy Susan Cafe in Cannon Beach (below) offers seafood as well as homemade soups and desserts. Co-owner Maureen Dooley-Sroufe serves up coffee and breakfast.

Lone beachcomber strolls a deserted beach in Ecola State Park. Oregon shores yield booty from afar, such as Japanese fishing floats, flotsam from shipwrecks, and messages in bottles. New treasures wash in with each storm. Armed with shovel and net bag, Gary Hansen (opposite) hunts living treasures, razor clams, at low tide on Seaside Beach. As he strikes the sand with the shovel, the clams burrow deeper, alerting Gary where to dig.

PAGES 194-195: "I beheld the grandest and most pleasing prospects which my eyes ever surveyed," wrote explorer Capt. William Clark about the Tillamook area coastline in 1806, an assessment still echoed today by many who visit this alluring hideaway.

IRA BLOCK

Notes on Contributors

IRA BLOCK has contributed to Society publications since 1975. In 1979, he traveled some 20,000 miles photographing *Back Roads America: A Portfolio of Her People.*

A onetime Air Force pilot, MATT BRADLEY has photographed three articles for NATIONAL GEOGRAPHIC and has contributed to four previous Special Publications.

Formerly with *U.S. News & World Report,* STEPHEN R. BROWN has photographed three stories for TRAVELER. This is his first Special Publications assignment.

MIKE CLEMMER has been a photojournalist for the past 21 years. His work has appeared in WORLD and several Society books, including *America's Wild Woodlands.*

One of the chief photographers for the Alaska pipeline, GEORGE HERBEN has contributed to several Society publications, including *Alaska's Magnificent Parklands.*

Before becoming a free lance, writer ERIK LARSON spent five years on the staff of the *Wall Street Journal.* This is his first assignment for Special Publications.

Since joining the Society staff in 1961, photographer GEORGE F. MOBLEY has traveled the world. His photographs of China, Africa, India, and other countries illustrate numerous magazine articles and books.

A Society staff member since 1976, senior writer THOMAS O'NEILL is the author of the Special Publications *Back Roads America* and *Lakes, Peaks, and Prairies: Discovering the United States-Canadian Border.*

Senior writer CYNTHIA RUSS RAMSAY has traveled widely since joining the Society staff in 1966. Her byline appears in many books, including *Splendors of the Past, Nature's World of Wonders,* and *Our Awesome Earth.*

Photographer SCOTT RUTHERFORD has contributed several articles to NATIONAL GEOGRAPHIC and TRAVELER. This is his first assignment for Special Publications.

JENNIFER C. URQUHART, who joined the Society staff in 1971, has written chapters for several Special Publications. Jenny has also written articles for TRAVELER and is the author of the children's book *Animals That Travel.*

Acknowledgments

The Special Publications Division is grateful to the organizations and individuals named or quoted in the text and to those cited here for their assistance during the preparation of this book: Chambers of Commerce in Nantucket and Vineyard Haven, Mass., Cannon Beach and Depoe Bay, Ore., and St. Thomas, U.S. Virgin Islands; Tourist Offices in Christiansted, St. Croix, USVI, and Road Town, Tortola, British Virgin Islands; Dr. Ewart Baldwin, William Binnewies, John and Patty Brissenden, John Corbett, Harry W. Crosby, Mrs. E. E. Daniel, Perry Davis, Jim Dice, Dwight Diller, Jean Drinkwine, David Fisk, Dennis Frye, Donald E. Giles, Brenda Goeres, Kevin and Tersa Keblaitis, Nis Kildegaard, Robert Lolmaugh, John Markwell, George Massie, Jeanne Mozier, Carole Q. Peters, Ted Scott, Gerry Searle, Craig See, Doris Simmons, Debby Stevenot, Warren Strycker, Joe Tecko, Mary Anna Wheat, Cathy Whittlesey, Carl Zambon.

Secluded beaches and other Caribbean charms lure visitors to tiny Buck Island, off St. Croix in the U.S. Virgins. An 850-acre national monument includes the entire island and surrounding coral reefs, where snorkelers follow underwater trails to view the colorful, varied sea life.
HARDCOVER: Boaters enjoy sparkling skies and crystal waters on St. John's Salomon Beach.

Library of Congress CIP Data
America's great hideaways.
  Bibliography: p.
  Includes index.
  1. United States—Description and travel—1981–   —Guidebooks.   2. North America—Description and travel—1981–—Guidebooks.   I. National Geographic Society (U.S.). Special Publications Division.   II. Title.
E158.A584   1986   917'.04538   86-12521
ISBN 0-87044-586-3 (regular edition)
ISBN 0-87044-591-X (library edition)

Composition for *America's Great Hideaways* by National Geographic's Photographic Services, Carl M. Shrader, Director, Lawrence F. Ludwig, Assistant Director. Printed and bound by Holladay-Tyler Printing Corp., Rockville, Md. Film preparation by Catherine Cooke Studio, Inc., New York, N.Y. Color separations by the Lanman Progressive Company, Washington, D.C.; Lincoln Graphics, Inc., Cherry Hill, N.J.; and NEC, Inc., Nashville, Tenn.

INDEX

Boldface indicates illustrations.

Additional Reading

Readers may consult the *National Geographic Index* for related articles and refer to the following books: Marje Blood, *Exploring the Oregon Coast by Car;* Elizabeth Carter, *Canoeing and Kayaking in Florida;* Eugenia H. Connally, *Wilderness Parklands in Alaska;* Alfred Eisenstaedt and Henry Beetle Hough, *Martha's Vineyard;* Esther Fraser, *The Canadian Rockies: Early Travels and Explorations;* Erle Stanley Gardner, *Off the Beaten Track in Baja;* Hoefer, Lueras, and Chung, *Hawaii;* J.S. Holliday, *The World Rushed In: The California Gold Rush Experience;* Peggy Larson, *The Deserts of the Southwest;* Dick Mackay, *Nantucket Whole Island Catalog II;* George Moses, *Minnesota in Focus;* National Geographic Society, *Alaska's Magnificent Parklands, America's Atlantic Isles, America's Spectacular Northwest, Isles of the Caribbean, The Great Southwest;* Lois O'Connor, *A Finger Lakes Odyssey;* Brian Patton, ed., *Tales From the Canadian Rockies;* Robert L. Reid, ed., *A Treasury of the Sierra Nevada;* C.R. Roseberry, *From Niagara to Montauk;* Gardner Soule, *The Long Trail;* John A. Williams, *West Virginia: A Bicentennial History.*